POEMS

OF

SENTIMENT AND IMAGINATION,

WITH

Dramatic and Descriptive Pieces.

BY

FRANCES A. AND METTA V. FULLER.

NEW YORK:
A. S. BARNES & CO., PUBLISHERS,
NO. 51 JOHN STREET.
1851.

STEREOTYPED BY BANER AND PALMER,
201 William Street., corner of Frankfort, N. Y.

TO OUR DEAR MOTHER,

THIS,

Our First Volume,

IS

GRATEFULLY AND AFFECTIONATELY

Inscribed.

AUTHORS' PREFACE.

In ushering to the world of letters this book of thoughts and feelings, germed in the seclusion of a dreamy youth, the authors, it may be conceived, had not the fear of criticism in their minds, else, perhaps, polish and elaboration might have insured more finished compositions. Many of the poems now collected have before appeared through various literary mediums, and to alter or remodel is a distasteful as well as difficult task. It is easy even now to perceive the crudeness which it will require years of thought and experience to mould into a pure and elevated style; but for this work, it is asked of friends and critics, that, viewing it as the first fruit-offering of young hearts, they "with all its faults will love it still."

CONTENTS.

POEMS BY FRANCES A. FULLER.

POEMS BY METTA VICTORIA FULLER.

POEMS

BY FRANCES A. FULLER.

THE VOLUNTEER.

"Night hath made many bards, she is so lovely;"
But in the South's bright clime, of which I speak,
Night holds her court in glory. There she seems
To center all her softness and her light,
To make a focus of her loveliness;
And weaving in her dark veil myriad stars,
Blending their clear light with the softer beams
Of a most queenly moon, she strives to make
Atonement for the burning glare of day
With such a world of sweetness, poetry,
Flowers and perfume, witching light and shade,
Murmuring music, and soft falling dew,
As would have made a gala-night in Eden.
'Twas such a night as this, when o'er the earth
Stole every form of loveliness. The air
Sighed faintly with its burden of perfume,
And lifted on its wings the golden light
That streamed in waving pennons, fluttering
To the slow motion of some zephyr's wing.
Night's sensitive flowers had oped their starry eyes,
Undaunted by the moon's love-looking face,
And breathed their sweetness to the gentle wind
As coyly, yet as tenderly as girls
Whisper the first confession of their love.
All 'neath that sky was loveliness and peace,

Save where upon a wide and grove-bound plain
Lay the white tents of soldiers, and the drum
Beat the tattoo that warned them to repose,
Or the guard's sleepless vigil.
But *one* heard
The solemn beat of that tattooing drum,
To whom e'en weariness, and a day's toil
Beneath a torrid sun, could not win sleep.
He with the form towering and graceful,
And yet delicate—a boy in seeming.
The high pale brow, and the dark wavy hair,
Have a fine placid beauty; but the eye,
Save now, when tears are in it, has a fire
That makes the face seem fearful; and the lip,
Used to compression, has the bent of scorn—
A dark, fierce, bitter scorn—the scorn of hate.
But he is softened now; the scene, the time,
Have found a soul-spring in his stormy being;
And thoughts have come of a time like to this,
When he was sinless, and when love first fell
Upon his wayward heart. But like the dew
Within the calyx of some noxious flower,
It but distilled its poison, and his soul
Steeped deadliness within it. She he loved
Was like a star to him, she was so pure;
A fair young creature, with a quiet face,
And an eye clear as heaven, and as starry.
Yet was there beauty in her quietness;
As a lake, when 'tis waveless, looks most deep.
And her he loved—and 'twas perchance because
That she was so unlike him that she gave
More scope to his impetuous nature than would one
Who could be wild as he was. But he loved—
No, worshiped had been better said than loved—
For he had set her image in his heart,
And bowed him down like an idolater,
In impious adoration, ere he knew
Or hardly cared to know, that she would look

With warmth upon his passion. He dream'd not
That one so gentle could turn from the power
Of the same spell that bound *him.* But he found,
Too late to save his peace, her heart preferred
The homage of another. Then sprang forth
The demon in his nature. With a howl
He fled through night and darkness, recking not
Of men's thoughts or of danger. On he went,
Gnashing his teeth with rage, and hissing out
Curses upon his rival. Thus was spent
The first burst of his fury; then there came
A darker spirit, with a deadlier aim,
And counseled with the demon in his heart,
And it consented. Ere the stars had looked
Upon another meeting of the lovers,
One slept in death; and he, the assassin, stole
A look of triumph on his bloody work,
Then fled to *serve his* COUNTRY! He saw not
His bitterest revenge, the helpless grief
Of her who died of madness.

'Twas this, the story of her pitiful death,
And her long suffering first, that woke once more
The inner wells of feeling, and drew tears,
The first had moistened his wild, burning eye
For many terrible months. For hours he wept,
Till drowsiness, like a nepenthe, soothed
His wakened feeling, and sleep came with dreams.
In thought he wandered weary o'er the earth,
Seeking a place to hide himself from men;
But all the world was peopled, and the crowds
That met him everywhere, all looked on him
With their astonished eyes, as if to say,
"How! art thou here?" and children shrunk away,
And peered at him from out each window nook,
Mocking at him, yet fearing to be seen.
Nowhere was solitude; he had grown old
Seeking for rest that he might never find;

And now he sat him on a church's steps,
Fainting from utter helplessness and want.
A crowd swept by him. On, with stately step,
Came a procession, headed by a bier
Shrouded with sable drapery of grief.
They were the first that had not heeded him,
And wondering with a strange happiness
If he had not been dreaming all his woe,
He followed the procession to the vault,
Beneath the marble pavement of the church,
And saw them lift the coffin-lid once more
Ere its pale inmate perished from their sight;
When lo! the corpse sat upright, and its hand,
Wasted and fleshless, pointed straight at him;
And the eyes gazed with terror; and the lips
Breathed a low wail of fear, and, quivering, closed;
Then the corpse sank back motionless again.
Enough for him. Even the haggard face,
And hair more white than silver, could not make
His heart deceive him. 'Twas *her* altered form.
The crowd turned to him when that bony hand
Pointed him out, and when surprise was past,
Rushed with a yell upon him. Thus he woke.
The morning drum proclaimed the time was near
When deadly contest between foe and foe
Required his soldier's spirit, and he shook
The influence from him of that dreadful dream,
And went forth to the struggle.

Night came again, and closed the scene of strife;
But not a night of beauty. 'Twould have mocked
Too much the desolation of the blood-stained earth,
Had beaming skies looked on it. Flying clouds
Belted the moon with mourning; and the wind
Moaned hoarsely through the tree-tops, that bent low
To evade its rising fury. In this hour
A dying wretch uplifted his pale face,
Praying for that wherewith to quench his thirst,

And cool his burning fever; and there came
In answer to his prayer a gentle hand
Bearing the draught of water; and a voice
Of sympathy in foreign accent bade
The sufferer take courage, and revive.
But death was at his heart, and gasping out
The name of her whom he had doubly murdered,
He quivered in his agony, and died.
And the kind Mexic woman, with a sigh,
Kept on her way in mercy, giving life
Alike to foe or countryman; and all
Raised their weak hands, and blessed her as she passed.

THE POST-BOY'S SONG.

The night is dark, and the way is long,
And the clouds are flying fast;
The night-wind sings a dreary song,
And the trees creak in the blast:
The moon is down in the tossing sea,
And the stars shed not a ray;
The lightning flashes fearfully,
But I must on my way.

Full many a hundred time have I
Gone o'er it in the dark,
Till my faithful steeds can well descry
Each long familiar mark:
Withal, should peril come to-night,
God have us in his care!
For without help, and without light,
The boldest well beware.

Like a shuttle thrown by the hand of fate,
  Forward and back I go;
Bearing a thread to the desolate
  To darken their web of woe;
And a brighter thread to the glad of heart,
  And a mingled one to all;
But the dark and the light I can not part,
  Nor alter their hues at all.

Now on, my steeds! the lightning's flash
  An instant gilds our way;
But steady! by that dreadful crash
  The heavens seemed rent away.
Soho! here comes the blast anew,
  And a pelting flood of rain;
Steady! a sea seems bursting through
  A rift in some upper main.

'Tis a terrible night, a dreary hour,
  But who will remember to pray
That the care of the storm-controlling power
  May be over the post-boy's way?
The wayward wanderer from his home,
  The sailor upon the sea,
Have prayers to bless them where they roam—
  Who thinketh to pray for me?

But the scene is changed! up rides the moon
  Like a ship upon the sea;
Now on, my steeds! this glorious noon
  Of a night so dark shall be
A scene for us; toss high your heads
  And cheerily speed away;
We shall startle the sleepers in their beds
  Before the dawn of day.

Like a shuttle thrown by the hand of fate,
  Forward and back I go;

Bearing a thread to the desolate
 To darken their web of woe;
And a brighter thread to the glad of heart,
 And a mingled one for all;
But the dark and the light I can not part,
 Nor alter their hues at all.

THE DESERTED CITY.

I HAD been weeping—not the April dew
That leaves the heart the lighter for the shedding;
But drops of anguish, from a fountain full
Of bitter waters—troubled, too, and deep.
Till the moon rose to the horizon's brim
And looking o'er the earth with a calm smile,
Went on her peaceful way among the stars,
I sat with brow bared to the balmy breath
Of the soft breeze of evening, as it came
Whispering around me with a lulling song,
Kissing most tenderly my fevered brow,
Wooing the agony from my wild pulse,
And striving by its blandishments to steal
My soul away into forgetfulness.
And when the moon, like a sweet white-robed mother,
In all her pensive loveliness uprose,
And went forth, with her still white feet, among
The stars, her sleeping children, with a smile
Of mingled majesty and matchless love,
I raised my eyes as a lone orphan would,
Longing for the great bliss of tenderness;
And lo! the light of her angelic face
Was bent upon me—sad, but oh, so sweet!
And by degrees my anguish wore away,

And the tumultuous throbbing of my pulse
Grew low, subdued, and gentle; and I breathed
My sorrow out in sighs, that were no more
The deep convulsiveness of bitter grief.
And by and by the earth and I, her child,
Slumbered in peace beneath the gentle reign
Of the fair queen of bright dominioned night.
But still I deemed that I was by my casement,
And that there lay beneath me, in the light
Of the full midnight moon, a lovely city;
A city beautiful with trees and fountains,
And works of grace and splendor, and high domes;
Palaces glittering in the moon's bright rays,
Gleaming like alabaster; and broad streets
Paved costlily with marble in mosaic,
But overgrown with grass and trailing weeds.
The spires, and palace-towers, and monuments,
Gleamed brightly in the moonlight, but rank moss
Waved from the terraces to the swaying wind,
With a low, rustling sound, and full of woe.
No print of feet was seen on any door-stone,
Not from one casement streamed the light of lamps,
But every where had desolation stalked,
Till not even one of all these palaces
Owned lord or serf—but all were tenantless.
And I alone was the sole living thing
That breathed within the city's silent walls.
The loneliness was awful; I stole down
From my still chamber to the trackless street,
And onward still, from palace unto palace,
Entering each by the wide-opened doors,
Whose hinges were no longer free to turn;
And flitting ghostlily from room to room,
Pursued by phantom fears, I hastened on.
The moonlight checkered the cold marble floors,
And gleamed upon rich velvet, and high walls
Hung with dark paintings, frescoing their sides;
And glittered on large mirrors, that had not

Reflected life for many a silent year.
Volumes unoped were lying mouldering,
Vases whose flowers crumbled to the touch,
Gems and rich ornaments, were scattered round,
All useless and neglected. In a hall,
Decked for the revel of the bright and young,
Were lamps all garlanded with withered flowers,
And tables spread with rich untasted wines,
And burdened with their weight of services.
My fears grew tremulous, and I sat down,
Reclining on the velvet now become
Faded and ruined for the want of use,
And tried to think of all that had been here;
But ever and anon my fancy made
A sound to startle me where none could be;
And forms were flitting in the twilight dim,
Caused by the moon's uncertain brilliancy
Of grotesque shapelessness, and mocking me
With looks of grim defiance, 'till my brain
Grew wild with terror, and I screamed, to make
A real sound to fright away my fears.
But echo, waked from such long slumbering,
Gave back a hollow and hoarse moaning voice
That made the place more awful than before.
And shrieking in my terror, I sprang up,
Running from room to room in my despair,
Until from weariness I paused, at length,
Within a chamber vast and desolate,
Hung with a solemn tapestry of black.
Upon a throne of marble, plain and firm,
A giant skeleton sat stark and stiff,
Holding a scepter in his bony hand.
This, then, the prince of all this fair outlay
Of wealth—and loneliness! I mused—and woke,
My head reclining on some few old letters
I had been reading as the twilight faded.
How like this city had my heart become!
Once it was fair, and garnished by Love's hand;

But Love was banished, and the monarch *Self*,
Had died of his own loneliness. Once more
I vowed to call Love from his exilement,
And make the city all his own again.

FOREST SPIRITS; OR, THE WOODS OF THE WEST.

Know ye the shades that inhabit our woods,
The spirits that dwell in their deep solitudes?
Have ye not heard them away in the shade,
And listened with awe to the sounds that they made?
And have ye not trembled with fear, when alone
Ye have heard in the forest their low solemn tone?
Have ye not heard, when the tempest was nigh,
Their voice in the wood like a mortal's wild cry?
And did ye not hear, when the storm was allayed,
Their low wailing sigh stealing out o'er the glade?
'Twas the voices of spirits—I know where they dwell,
And oft have I listened the tales that they tell.

Far away, in the forest's impervious gloom,
Where the birds never sing, and the flowers never bloom,
Where the darkness is deep as the midnight can be,
And the owl hoots all day in his horrible glee;
Where the snake and the lizard crawl over the mould,
And feast in the darkness, the damp, and the cold—
It is here that the spirits that shriek and that moan,
Retreat when the wrath of the tempest hath gone.
And the tales that they tell are of wrath and of blood;
Of the fight on the plain, and the chase on the flood;
Of the whoop, and the yell, and the death of the brave,
And of woman's wild wail o'er the warrior's grave;
O their voice is as wild as the ocean-bird's cry,
As it shrieks o'er the wave, and rings up to the sky!

But in the deep shade of the violet dells,
Are the spirits that tell us of lovers' farewells;
And we hear them at night when the flower-oping breeze
Just rustles the boughs of the leaf-laden trees.
They tell of the love of the dark forest maid,
Of the words that were said 'neath the willow-bough's shade;
Of the anger of rivals, the challenge to fight,
Of the death of the brave, and the funeral rite;
Of the maiden's mad sorrow; and whispering wild,
They tell of the grief of the chief for his child—
That beneath the lake's waters, so dark and so deep,
The maiden sank down to her visionless sleep.
And the girls of the forest at evening brought flowers,
The fairest that grew in their wild woodland bowers,
And scattered them over the lake's silver breast,
And chanted a dirge that the spirit might rest.
But 'twas whispered the maiden came up from the wave,
To ramble at eve with her warrior brave;
And the spirits that dwell in the woods caught the tone
Of the maiden's low wail and the warrior's moan;
And still at this hour, when the breeze wanders by,
Breathe out in the forest their low mournful cry.

Have you not been where the silver beech flingeth
Its arms o'er the spot where the wood-fountain springeth?
Where the fern and the wild-flower bend o'er its brim
To gaze on their shadows so dark and so dim;
Where the moss like a carpet of velvet is spread,
And its roots are inwove with the bright golden thread;
Where the wintergreen berries like ruby-drops shine,
And the turf is embroidered with wild cypress vine;
Where the brave olden trees, towering up to the blue,
Let scarcely a glimpse of the golden day through;
Where the light is as soft as the orange-tree's bloom,
And the birds rarely sing, overpowered with perfume?
It was here that the tawny-browed queen of the wood
Came to dream of her love in the dim solitude;

And the spirits that watched o'er her slumbers repeat
In their low silver voices, so clear and so sweet,
A thousand soft murmurs, the tones of her love,
Like the gush of a fountain, the coo of a dove;
O their voice is as thrilling, their accent as wild,
As the heart and the dream of the dark forest child!

Know ye the spirits that dwell by the river
That rolleth its flood to the ocean forever;
That rusheth and roareth from mountain to plain,
'Till its thunder is lost in a sullen complain?
Have ye not stood where the torrent was breaking
Its tide on the rocks, till each echo awaking,
Hath joined in the chorus with torrent and river,
And lengthened the anthem forever and ever?
Have ye not been where the rivulet leapeth
On through the shade where the willow-bough weepeth,
Glancing along in its beautiful motion,
Till the river hath borne it away to the ocean?
Ah, there are spirits by brooklet and river,
Where the giant trees grow or the frail flowers quiver,
In the glen and the dell, by the lake and the fountain,
In the shadowy wood, on the pine-covered mountain—
Not a spot where the foot of the white man can tread,
But spirits are whispering tales of the dead.

Proud forests! ye stately old woods of the West,
In what glorious hues are your aged boughs drest!
How bravely ye stand in your gorgeous pride,
Decked out in the robes that old autumn hath dyed;
Yet my heart hath grown sadder by gazing on ye,
And list'ning the voices that sigh from each tree,
For they tell of the red man—the child of the wood—
And his form seems to rise in the dim solitude;
And now when the autumn winds sigh through the trees,
His voice haunts my ear with each swell of the breeze;
I hear his low call, and his step stealing by,
The twang of the bow, and the bird's sudden cry—

A thousand wild murmurings tremble in air,
And startle my spirit with thrillings of fear;
Yet I love the wild music for breathing the tone
Of ages gone by, and of races long flown.
Old forests! ye stand in your majesty yet,
Bearing proudly the seal by the Deity set;
First temples of God—where His presence still seems
To tremble like visions of angels in dreams;
Would that never thine echoes might wake to repeat
The voice of the white man, the tread of his feet;
For the shades which inhabit shall flee from thy dells,
And the shelter be torn from thy wild-springing wells;
And thy shadowy recesses, dim as the night,
Shall be oped to the glare of the summer-day's light;
And thy soft mossy glades, by the wood-blossom starred,
By the tramp of his footsteps be stricken and marred.
Where the pride of thy bosom now towers to the skies,
Shall a temple of fame in the future arise;
And man in the pride of his strength shall erase
Of the forest's wild grandeur each lingering trace.
Columbia's forests! how proudly ye wave
O'er the white man's domain, and the Indian's grave·
Yet do ye not mourn that the sons of thy shade
Have been driven away from the homes they had made?
Do not the wild spirits in glade, glen, and dell,
Echo mournfully over the Indian's farewell?
Or is it the farewell to man's first abode,
Murmuring still from thy branches, great wind-harp of God?

ELOISE.

Night, lovely nun, had donned her sable vail,
And softly as a dream had stolen forth
From evening's shadowy cloisters, and begun
To light her vestal fires in heaven's high vault.
When these were burning bright, she lifted up
The moon's great golden lamp to heaven's midst,
And shrinking from the light herself had made,
Fled to the shadows of the woods and hills,
To keep her holy vigil. The tired earth slept
Softly as girlhood, and the air was still
As infant's breathing, save when from the grove
Came the low murmur of dew-dripping trees,
And notes of night-birds singing to their loves.
But it was burdened with the sweets of flowers,
And the rich fragrance of magnolia trees,
That lifted their proud, lovely heads afar
Toward the brightness of the beaming sky,
As loving and imploring—as our souls
Go out in prayer to beauty, with a gush
Of holy tenderness we can not quell.

Amid the scene, the only unblest thing,
Walked Manhood, with his hot and painful pulse
Throbbing with scarce less fever even when
Night's holy presence chided his mad dreams.
He walked and mused; anon he flung his arms
With passionate vehemence; and low words,
Uttered with emphasis that thrilled the air,
Came from his writhing lips; and his bent head
Was lifted not toward heaven—as if he feared,
Or had forgot its beauty. Thus he strode,
Muttering his restless fancies to himself,
And making discord in night's silent hymn,
Till from the shadow of an orange grove

Flashed out a sudden vision; and a word
Like one fine note of music caught his ear:
"Alberto!"—but he started not with joy
At the sweet bidding. Sullenly he turned
And gazed in silence, till from very fear
Of this dark mood she fled into his arms,
And nestled timidly upon his breast,
And looked into his face, and spoke again
His name in softest accents: "My Alberto!"
Still did he gaze unmoved, until her tears
Forced from his lips their venom. "Eloise,
Once to have held thee thus within my arms
Would have been bliss like heaven's. But thou art false—
Most beautiful, but false." And with his gaze
Bent sternly on the pale and tearful face
Turned upward to his own, he pushed her back,
And folded up his arms.

"Art thou not mad,
Dearest Alberto; or is this a fraud,
Though strange and cruel, used to try my love?
Tell me if thou dost mean to test my truth."

"Thou hast no truth to prove, fair Eloise;
And I say thou art false, who loved thee most;
Then spare us both these feints and artful words.
I could forgive thee if thou didst not play
The actress with me now. And now I go;
But ere I go, I'll say I *do* forgive thee.
God bless thee, Eloise!"

"One moment stay!
Leave me not, or I die, this hour and here.
My senses are bewildered, and this seems
An ill-timed jest that you will soon explain.
You *can not* think me false. Oh, aught but this!
Tell me your love is altered, or protest
That you have never loved me: that would give

Strength to my pride, and I could live and smile;
But part not from me with the cruel charge
That *I* am the one perjured."

The stern man
Was softened for a moment, and he took
Those clasped hands in his own, and pressed a kiss
Upon the cold, white brow, and laid her head
Again upon his bosom. But the touch
Recalled his iron will. "Nay, Eloise,
Why should I trust thee? Has not all the world
Learned this before I murmured, while I was
The dupe of my own blindness? Do not think
I stoop to breathe reproaches. Never waste
A thought upon my fortunes; for I give
My heart henceforward to ambition's race,
And worship fame alone. Beauty's wiles
Shall never stay my footsteps—men shall be
The instruments of greatness to myself,
And I'll forget that ever I did dream
This vain and broken fancy of first love."

As if an adder coiled about her form,
She started from his arms. "Alberto, hear!
You charge my soul with falsehood for no cause
Save the world's idle babble; cruelly
You break asunder every tie that binds
My very life to yours. I will not say
Again that I am innocent, but turn
Your charge upon yourself; for never love
Coldly and calmly thus relinquished love.
I know the bane that has distilled this ruin.
Go, give your manhood to it! and when age
Comes with its weary heart and feeble pulse,
Weigh then what you have gained against your loss;
I can divine the balance. Go; farewell!"

Alberto gazed upon that hueless face,
With the dark, passionate eyes now bright with scorn,

And the lips ashen with the stifled pain,
And the proud form more peerless in its pride,
Till his brain swam with dizziness; yet turned
And followed his dark monitor, Ambition. * * *

A half-score years had fled. Within a room,
Where wealth and elegance combined with art
To make a home for genius, as are set
Rich gems in finest gold, reclined a man,
The master of the place. The silken lounge
Was placed beside a window, through which stole,
Waving the parted curtains, the sweet breath
Of the young spring-time; and it stirred his hair,
Dallying with the curls, until it brought
The memory of a time when a fair hand
Had parted those dark locks upon his brow,
And twined the jeweled fingers with their shreds,
While he pored over the time-honored tome
That fed his dreams of glory. And there came
Over his heart a yearning to behold
The idol of his youth, to which was given
All his heart knew of love. That one last scene,
Fraught with the destiny of both, came back
With strange distinctness; and a chilling dread
Haunted him like a specter.
Fame was won,
And wealth and honor; all he hoped and wished;
Yet he looked back upon a sea of strife;
And forward, a wide desert met his view;
And what at best was life? When all was won,
Then the desire was dead; and loathingly
He turned him from the spectacle that lay
Within the gilded temple he had sought.

Beneath the splendors of a southern sky,
A palace reared its walls. Stately and fair,
It rose amid a grove of flowering trees,
Whose perfume burdened all the sunny air.

Fountains gushed in the shade, and flowers bloomed,
And vines were clambering over trellised walks,
And balconies were radiant with bloom;
All things without were lovely; and within
Was a charmed dwelling; so much art,
With wealth and skill, had fashioned that was fair.
But one who came, paused at the outer gate,
And pondered long before he took his way
Toward the high-arched portal. There he paused,
And laid his hand upon his beating heart
To still its sickening tumult.
Menials bade
The stranger enter softly, for that death
Was then within their walls. He hushed his heart,
And questioned of them who had lately died;
And they told him this story: "She who lies
Shrouded in yonder chamber, has long been
Bereft of reason, though so sweet and kind,
And so majestic in her daily port,
That none except her household ever knew
The wildness of her fancies. But she had
A phantasy that some one, one Alberto,
Was gone upon a pilgrimage, from which
When he returned he'd claim her for his bride.
And so she planned this palace and these grounds,
And furnished all things to receive her love.
She had a portrait in a certain chamber,
Which she said was Alberto's; and a chair,
Fashioned luxuriously, was set beside
A table covered with the choicest books;
And here she sat sometimes with her guitar,
On a low ottoman, beside that chair,
And thought that she was listened to by him;
And would look up, and smile, and chide his frowns;
But this was only in her wildest moods.
At length her reason came, and she fell ill,
And wasted with consumption. But she died
In the room called Alberto's.

Our lady, sir,
Was very beautiful, and you can see
The corse, if you desire."
He followed them
To the dim chamber of the white-robed dead,
And saw them lift the pall, and then he spoke—
"*I* am Alberto; leave me here alone!"
Wondering, they turned away, and he knelt down
Beside the flower-strewn bier.
At eve they came
To rouse the stranger from his mournful watch;
But to their kind entreaties no reply
Came from the mourner's lips; and when they raised
His forehead from the bosom of the corse,
They quailed with terror, for he too was dead.
Her love had come at length, and Death had wed them!

DREAMINGS OF LIFE.

I SLEPT, and in my sleep I thought
That I was in a dream—
A dream so earnest and so strange,
That even now I deem
'Twas more than the vague phantasies
With which our slumbers teem.

I thought 'twas night—O such a night!
A night so strangely fair,
When the stars smile down so angel-like,
And through the lucid air
The moonbeams poured in a shining cloud
Like a mass of golden hair!

The shadows of the summer trees
  Made columns dark and long
Across the brightly sparkling turf,
  And their leaves kept up a song—
A song they'd learned of the dreamy brook
  That sung as it flowed along.

Oft have I heard that tune at night,
  As it came from the waving wood,
When the breeze was reveling 'mong the boughs,
  And stirring the solitude ;
And it ever filled my youthful heart
  With a wild and yearning mood.

I dreamed that I stood in a spot most like
  A place that I had seen,
With its waving wood on a moonlit bank,
  And turf of dewy sheen,
And its intertwining canopy,
  With the moon and stars between.

The river that glided at my feet,
  And trilled its murmured tone,
Had a sound like something I had heard
  In the blissful years agone ;
And I marveled how I reached that place,
  Yet never the change had known.

The long grass waved from the water's edge,
  And dipped in the silver tide ;
And its shadow laid on the glittering waves
  As the lashes of some young bride
Do droop o'er the clear, dark, shining well,
  Where her timid feelings hide.

I thought 'twas strange I was standing there,
  Alone with the midnight moon,

And a shuddering fear thrilled through my veins
As I listened the night-wind's tone ;
And as it sighed in my unbound hair,
I smothered a whispered moan.

But the vision that rose in the yellow air
Held my shuddering senses still ;
I could not speak, or breathe, or stir,
But a damp and deathly chill
Bound with its icy grasp my heart,
That it could not even thrill.

A ghostly form, with silver hair
Flowing down to his feet,
And a face so dark, and withered, and wild,
And eyes that I dared not meet—
So stony and cold they looked on me
From brows as white as sleet.

"Shall I show thee life?" he spoke at length,
But I answered not for fear ;
And a mocking smile played on his face,
So withered, and wild, and sere ;
And I closed my eyes for a moment, till
That look should disappear.

But when I looked, in its wonted tide
My blood flowed fast and free ;
And almost without knowing why
I laughed in my careless glee ;
And naught at all of the strange old man
Could my happy vision see.

I seemed to stand on that moonlit bank
With a form on either side,
Of friends I had known in girlhood's days
Ere either the world had tried—
Of a girl in her earliest loveliness,
And a boy in youth's first pride.

Her arms were twined about my form;
I looked into her eyes;
The light that shone in their starry depths
Was as clear as summer skies;
And her face had that pure spirit-look
That any sin defies.

Her dark curls laid upon my neck,
Her clear cheek to my own,
And her gentle breath perfumed the air
Like hyacinths half-blown;
While words of sweetest poetry
Wreathed with her music tone.

The proud boy marked her soft, low words;
His tones grew wild and deep,
And I felt the heart so near my own
More passionately leap,
And the warm blood to her rose-leaf cheek
In a swift torrent sweep.

And still we three held converse there,
Beneath the midnight moon,
Nor thought that the night was waning fast,
And the stars would very soon
Grow wan and pale in the misty air,
As if sinking in a swoon!

The scene was changed. In a vaulted hall
I sat amid a crowd,
And round me pressed an eager throng
Of the gifted and the proud;
And all to the might of eloquence
In quiet rapture bowed.

I almost hushed my breath to hear,
Yet strongly my heart beat;

And I dreamed it would be bliss to live
  Forever at *his* feet,
At the feet of him whose eloquence
  Was so strangely grand and sweet!

But a sudden thought dashed on my brain,
  The thought of that night in June,
When a boy stood on the river bank,
  Beneath the midnight moon;
And I knew the son of fame was he
  I had known in years agone!

Then I thought of the girl with the dreamy eyes,
  But ere my thoughts were shaped,
I seemed to stand beside a bier
  With sable velvet draped;
And a man knelt there in agony,
  Of which no sound escaped.

And I seemed to read the hidden past
  As it were from out a book;
I knew full well why that strong man
  In such mute anguish shook;
And I shrunk away from him, nor dared
  Upon his grief to look.

He was the boasted idol-shrine
  Round which a nation bowed;
And the wild acclaim of worshipers—
  The blinding incense-cloud—
Had hidden too long the idolater
  Now folded in her shroud.

Another change—and a noble man,
  With brow of kingly pride,
Trod proudly through a glittering throng
  With a fair girl by his side;
And I knew by her snowy vail and wreath
  She was a youthful bride.

I remembered the fair and shrouded form
  I had seen upon the bier,
And almost without knowing why,
  My spirit quailed with fear ;
And though I strove to be at ease
  I could not see or hear.

Once more I stood on that moonlit bank,
  And that old man gazed on me,
And his stony eyes shone with disdain
  As he asked " *Wouldst thou now see*
Another page in the book of life—
  A page filled out for thee ?"

I could not bide that old man's smile,
  It shone through the yellow air
With such a wild derisive gleam,
  And his eyes had such a stare—
A stare so frozen and icy cold
  That surely they could not glare.

Again my curdling blood stood still ;
  I struggled to even moan ;
The old man smiled a pitiful smile,
  And I sank into a swoon ;
Nor dreamed again, 'till from my sleep
  I was wakened by the tune
Of the night-wind in the waving wood,
  And the brightness of the moon.

KATE.

I know one—I wish you knew her,
  Dark-eyed, rose-lipped, darling Kate!
Many an eye's bright cynosure,
  Many a fond heart's star of fate.
Stately as the lily-blossom,
  And as queenly and as fair;
With no sin in her young bosom,
  On her brow no shade of care.

Should you see her you would love her;
  All who ever knew her do;
But I fear you can not move her
  To confess that she loves you.
For the little witch is wicked,
  In a pretty, harmless way,
And if you should seem tormented,
  Would delight to say you "nay."

Half-a-dozen dimples hover
  'Mong the roses on her cheek;
Should she smile, you'll soon discover
  How they play at hide-and-seek.
And her smile is just the fleetest,
  Brightest, most enchanting smile!
And her merry laugh the sweetest
  You will hear in many a mile.

From her pure and child-like forehead
  Many a dark-brown silken tress,
Simply and demurely braided,
  Still betrays her loveliness.
And the eyelids' long dark lashes
  Have a most provoking art,
Drooping when the soft eye flashes
  With the truth of her wild heart.

Should she let them smile upon you
With their own peculiar light,
Keep your heaviest armor on you,
For there's mischief in the sprite.
If you have the heart of human,
She will pilfer it away;
And so slyly, how the woman
Got it you could never say.

But with all is Kate the dearest,
Kindest little girl on earth;
With an eye and soul the clearest,
And the softest in their mirth.
Stately as the lily-blossom,
And as queenly and as fair,
With no sin in her young bosom,
On her brow no shade of care.

THE OLD MAN'S FAVORITE.

Do you ask where she has fled—
Fanny, with the laughing eyes?
Should I tell you "She is dead,"
You would mimic tears and sighs,
And pretend a sad surprise.

Yester-week, when you were here,
She was sitting on your knee,
Whispering stories in your ear
With an air of mystery,
And a roguish glance at me.

Fanny's heart was always light,
  Light and free as plumed bird;
When she glanced within our sight,
  Or her merry voice we heard,
  Music in our hearts was stirred.

Ask you still where Fanny hides?
  I will tell you by and by;
Look you where the river glides,
  In whose depths the shadows lie,
  Mingled of the earth and sky.

Fanny always loved that spot;
  There her favorite flowers grew—
Violet, Forget-me-not,
  And the Iris' gold and blue,
  With its pearly beads of dew.

Oft on the old rustic bridge,
  Made of supple boughs entwined,
Hanging from each margin's ridge
  Like a hammock in the wind,
  Fanny fearlessly reclined.

And she told me, while her eyes
  Filled with tears of childish bliss,
That she could see Paradise,
  From her rocking resting-place,
  Mirrored in the river's face;

That she saw the tall trees wave;
  Bright-winged birds among their bowers;
And a river that did lave
  Banks o'ergrown with fairest flowers,
  And a sky more bright than ours.

Then she asked, with such a smile
  As an angel face might wear,
If she watched a long, long while,

She should see her mother there,
Walking in the groves so fair.

When to soothe the child I said,
She should see mamma in heaven,
To that frail old bridge she sped
As if wings to her were given;
And—but look—you see 'tis riven!

Ah! you start—your looks are wild—
Calm yourself old man, I pray;
Fanny was an angel child,
And 'tis well she's gone away
To her Paradise so gay!

QUEEN MARY'S LOVER.

Thine the warrant, lovely Mary, thine the hand that writes my doom!
Thou shalt see how dies a lover when his mistress opes his tomb;
Matchless Mary, divine Mary, Love's and Beauty's peerless queen,
Death has not a pang to daunt me, not a terror that can haunt me;
What *thou* sendest to me, Mary, I can meet with smiling mien.

Call me not an impious traitor! he who loves so well as I
Hell nor heaven could make disloyal, though his madness make him die.
Heaven preserve thee when I perish other friends that are as true;
Traitors' gilded snares *may* find thee, and their cunning toils may bind thee,
Then may love like mine, O Mary, live to show its truth to you.

Thou hast saved thine honor, Mary ; thou hast kept thy stainless name ;
Be my loyal blood the voucher for thy spotlessness of fame ;
But its worth will be diminished by the price which thou hast given,
And thy secret heart rebelling, to thy soul will ere be telling
That thy truest lover waits thee on the confines of his heaven.

Was I a traitor, O blest Mary, when I saw thee kneeling there
In thy chamber's holy silence, sending up thy evening prayer ?
Not the holy Virgin Mother could more pure or glorious seem ;
And when from thy lips ascending, my name with thy God's was blending—
Mary, Mary, as immortal as my soul will be that dream!

Did I wrong her whom I worshiped, was her beauty made profane ?
Let my life-blood pay the penance, and remove the blushing stain;
Still the daring sin committed which the queen can not forgive,
In thy woman's soul repenting, finds a generous relenting,
Which while it would slay the subject, would still bid the lover live.

God protect thee, beauteous princess, when the faithful are no more,
God's guiding angels pilot thee to Time's eternal shore ;
Though thy subject, Mary, fears not death, his heart doth sorely bleed,
For the future opes before him, and the prophet's vail falls o'er him,
And he sees for thee, sweet, hapless queen, a " time and hour of need."

The sullen bell is tolling that calls me to my doom;
Another morning's sun will shine upon thy lover's tomb;
I see thee at thy casement high, thy face bedewed with tears—
O fare-thee-well, my soul's bright queen, this sight divine that I have seen,
Of Mary weeping at my death, is worth a life of years!

A REVERIE.

Not from fancy's land of wonders
Come the dreams that haunt my brain,
But from out the past's dim chambers
Glide anon the shadowy train.
On each pale and solemn visage
Is some old remembrance prest,
Some old memory that hath lingered
Ever fadeless in my breast.

And as troop on troop of visions
Through thought's silent halls defile,
Like the ancient ghosts that wander
Through some lone cathedral aisle.
New-born fancies mix and mingle
With the old familiar throng,
And the Past and Present meeting,
Form the river-tide of song.

Dreams of present have no power,
And no grandeur like the past;
Glory borrows its enchantment
From the distance it is cast;
But the present is the wizard
That can break oblivion's seal,
And the "dead past's dead" unburied,
By a magic word reveal.

Life has many hidden currents,
Like the cave-streams of the earth,
Flowing deep and strong in secret,
Ne'er betraying bourne or birth;
But the flood in darkness wandering
With no flower upon its way,
Has its course 'mong richer treasures
Than have met the blaze of day.

Light that sometimes shines upon it
  Finds it deep, and pure, and cold;
And the starry gleam reflected,
  Leaves no bosom secret told.
In my spirit's depths are hidden
  Treasures gathered from all life:
Pearls of thought, and gold of feeling,
  Moveless with the current's strife.

In life's lively panorama,
  Looking for what is to be,
We forget to note the present
  Ere the changing phantoms flee;
But as clouds by tempests driven
  Scatter rain-drops as they fly,
Many golden sands have fallen
  Where they must forever lie.

In *my* heart the silver treble
  Of these broken notes of song,
Makes no discord in the music
  As it flows in waves along;
For the spirit of my dreaming
  Sings me all the missing notes,
And the strain to you so broken
  Perfect to my hearing floats.

THE POET'S HARP OF SORROWS.

Thou hast been silent long, harp of my sorrows,
I had thought ne'er to touch thy chords again!
But grief closed in the heart such sternness borrows,
It is relief to waken thy complain;
And I have yearned to lay my heart on thee,
And let its throbbings wake a symphony.

I have a vision in my heart—
A vision of years long gone by—
And from almost oblivion start
A thousand links of memory.
I see a dimly smiling band
Far back upon the stream of time;
And friendship's wreath from hand to hand
Links sunniest flowers of sunny clime.

I see them faintly though so near;
I gaze into their smiling eyes;
And from their soft warm lips I hear
The gushing of old melodies.
But they are passing; as I gaze
The light fades from each smiling brow;
Unlike that dream of by-gone days,
A specter-band glides by me now.

My eyes are dim with unshed tears
That burn like fire, but will not flow;
My vision hath recalled the years,
The light-winged, bright-hued long ago.
I hear the caroling of birds,
And murmur of a gurgling stream,
A low sweet laugh, and pleasant words,
And eyes long closed with brilliance beam.

I seem to feel the fragrant breath
  From bright, sweet lips, now pale and cold;
And forms come from the land of death
  To cluster round me as of old.
And one most fair of that fair band
  Smiles in my face with her pure eyes,
And the warm touch of her soft hand
  Thrills me with long-gone ecstasies.

Art thou too fled? In my embrace
  I clasp naught but the viewless air;
I gaze not in thy smiling face,
  O where art thou, my sweet bride, where?
Dost call me with thy gentle tone?
  And yet I can not follow thee!
I see thee not—I am alone;
  O come again, sweet bride, to me.

O wail, my harp it was a dream—
  A sweet deception, blessing me,
And passing as a cloud-rent beam
  Of sun upon a troubled sea.
Thy trembling chords may sadly shake,
  My heart-strings quiver like thine own,
And by their tension soon must break,
  Then breathe for me thy pensive moan.

Not yet, not yet; O cease not yet,
  Though sad the "burden of thy song;"
The restless spirit soon will set
  That hath disturbed thy chords so long.
What strains! O never had thy strings
  So much of ravishment as this;
I hear the rustling swoop of wings—
  My bride! O Death, thou comest in bliss!

DARKNESS.

I sit in the darkness all alone.
And list to the night-wind's whispered moan,
That is not as sad as my spirit's tone,
Nor any thing else can be;
For in this starless, moonless night,
With not a ray save the spirit's light,
I am musing o'er leaves, some sad, some bright,
In the book of memory.

A thousand dim forms around me glide,
And circle me in on every side,
And their presence urges the burning tide
Of thought upon my soul.
A fever is scorching heart and brain,
And burning in every throbbing vein,
And sudden thrills of a wild, fierce pain
Are mocking all control.

It is but my troubled dream, I know;
But the very darkness seems to glow,
And the stars to wander to and fro,
With a red and fiery gleam.
O for a ray of the blessed light,
To break the gloom of this fearful night,
And banish this vision from my sight,
And waken me from my dream.

I did not think, when I sat me here,
That the night would seem so dark and drear,
Or the air so full of forms of fear;
But I wished to sit and think,
In the breathless stillness of the night,
Of a lofty being, pure and bright,
Who had taught my spirit of the might
Of his own soul to drink.

And I dared to think that there might be
In the future's unseen treasury
A long-craved boon reserved for me,
The blessed boon of love!
But the past came up before mine eyes,
And I saw in dim succession rise
A thousand older memories,
Each one with sadness wove.

And a shadow o'er my spirit come,
And darker grew the midnight gloom,
And wilder, busier grew the hum
Of voices from the past;
Till I yielded up my hope in fear,
And shuddered in the darkness drear,
Too wildly sad to weep a tear—
To hope it might not last.

And still I sat when hope was dead,
And did not dare to raise my head,
For fear the vision was not fled,
Until a single star
Burst from the night-clouds' gloomy maze,
And broke on my bewildered gaze
In one intense and glorious blaze,
And darkness fled afar.

BEAUTY.

I have seen a gay, young, volatile creature,
With a form graceful as Hebe's, and a smile
Full of all winning witcheries; and features
Blended to such pure symmetry, that while
You strove to tell where most of beauty laid,
The delicate whole mingled in one soft shade,
With violet eyes, and drooping lids that looked

Like a soft pearl-cloud on the summer sky,
  And fair, smooth brow where purity seemed booked
Never to be erased ; and lips that vie
  With the young rosebud, that ever and anon
  Parted with smiles and snatches of sweet song ;
And hair bright as a gold-edged cloud, that hung
  In rippled ringlets round the soft, white neck,
And o'er the carmine of the young cheek flung
  A richer glow, such as tints from shadows take.
A form all symmetry, with delicate feet,
  And pretty dimpled hands and rounded arms,
And motions full of graces, such as meet
  To make perfection in one lovely form ;
And I did love her that she was to me
The witching embodiment of poetry.

And I knew one of a less lovely face,
  With form less fairy-like and beautiful,
With motions not so full of perfect grace,
  But whose chief charm was loveliness of soul !
Yet she *was* beautiful ; you should have seen
  The soft eye lighten, and the restless lip,
Tremulous with lofty sentiment, and been
  A listener to the glowing thoughts that leap
From the deep-welling fountains of her heart,
And watched the play of feelings as they'd start,
  Bringing the eloquent blood to her fair brow,
Deep'ning the color in her tell-tale eye,
  And blending her whole being in the glow
That wraps her spirit in such ecstasy.
  Then had you known what 'tis to feel the charm
Of all that's beautiful in our fair earth ;
  For her mind fed on loveliness, nor form,
Real nor spiritual, that has its birth,
  But was familiar to her delicate eye,
Until her spirit became poetry !
  And *her* I loved for beauty that is given
  To make us less of earth and more of heaven.

ONE OF OUR POETS.

Oft my fancy draws the picture, and for evermore he seems
Sitting silent in his chamber, brooding o'er his wondrous dreams;
Sitting motionless and weaving visions in his mighty brain—
Visions soft, and pure, and glowing, and with scarce an earthly stain—
Weaving into them his being, all its pleasures and its pain.

Coyly through the open casement steals the fragrant air of June,
Humming to itself the murmur of the woodland's pleasant tune;
Lifting up the silken curtain, through which comes the ruby tinge
Glowing in the chamber's twilight, toying with the golden fringe,
Prisoning the window-roses in its tassel-tangled swinge.

Fitful gleams of yellow sunlight flash across the velvet floor,
As the breeze in rising gladness lifts the curtain more and more,
And a smile seems stealing over the dim faces in the room,
'Till the pictured wall looks breathing through the soft and dreamy gloom,
Antique jewels seem to sparkle, and to wave the bending plume.

Nothing cares the silent dreamer that those pictures, old and dim,
Give more sense of life and motion to the gazer's eye than him;
Little heeds he sun or shadow, pleasant sounds or fragrant air;
He is in a world whose visions are a thousand times more fair,
Musing, speechless with enchantment, on the glorious beauties there.

More and more the curtain flutters, and upon the dreamer's hair
Falls the crimson glow of sunset, resting in a halo there;
On a brow so proud and pensive fitly placed the glory seems—
Looking like the lingering radiance borrowed in his land of dreams,
Broken, as the curtain flutters, into bright and changing gleams.

But anon the sun is setting, and the breeze has died away,
And the curtain and the sunbeam cease to quiver and to play,
And the spell so deeply woven round the dreamer seems to part,
Till the tide of life comes rushing faster from his fettered heart,
And his own unconscious murmurs wake him with a sudden start.

Hard upon his fevered eyelids presses he his trembling hand,
While a troop of white-winged visions vanish at his sad command;
Still he murmurs lightly to them, whispers to them o'er and o'er,
As he paces, in the twilight, noiselessly the chamber floor,
Murmuring ever, like a river, one same sound, and that *Lenore!*

Talking to his love in heaven, she who never leaves his side,
Hovering near, a winged spirit, still his angel and his bride;
Counting ceaselessly the hoarded treasures of his memory's store;
Burning out his heart in incense at the shrine he loved of yore,
Haunted by the "rare and radiant" maiden of his heart, *Lenore.*

A DUET.

MIRIAM BY FRANCES A., AND SYBIL BY METTA V. FULLER.

"There's a strange glow upon thy cheek to-day,
And an unnatural luster in thine eye;
And often o'er thy red lip's restless play,
The mournful tones steal forth and quivering die.
Miriam, thy glance doth startle me as strange,
There is such deep intenseness in its gaze;
Surely thy heart hath felt some sudden change—
Some heavy sorrow on thy spirit lays."

"Nay, mark not that the varying tide of thought
Hath taken, for once, more than its usual glow
Of ever-burning sadness: it is naught;
Then do not pain thy breast with thoughts of woe.
True, my cheek burns, but with mere earnestness,
The force of feelings in my heart untold—
Thoughts which I cherish not, nor can repress,
Not of wild sorrow, nor yet calmly cold."

"Ah, sister! is this all? Thou canst not hide
The secret sadness wearing life away;
The bitterness that in thy heart doth hide,
Dwelling in its still depths by night and day.
I tell thee I have heard thee in thy sleep
Murmuring strange, mournful words, that ever seem
So low and yet so wild, they make me weep
To think thy heart is breaking in thy dream."

"Do I then murmur in my sleep to thee,
Betraying the sad fancies in my brain?
'Sleep hath its own world'—reality
Thou shouldst not link with its unreal pain.
Sybil, dear sister, lay thy cheek to mine—
Talking of grief has even made me sad;
Whisper of love—no other love but thine!
And talk to me as though you deemed me glad."

"Ah, my own Miriam! has no other love
No whisper—no unutterable thrill—
Has thy warm heart, o'er-freighted like the dove,
With riches of affection, now grown still?
Surely the past, the bright, the lovely past,
Hath dreamy tales of love, and life, and bliss;
You do not deem such joys too bright to last—
Think of those hours and they will brighten this."

"Talk not of *love!* there's that within my heart
Whereon it falls as living fire would fall

Upon an unclosed wound; and memories start
Fearful as specters from beneath the pall
Of the unburied dead! no more, no more!
Never say aught again to me of bliss,
Since it is coupled with the empty lore
Of earth's vain love—away, away with this."

"O Miriam, hush! it frightens me to mark
The chilling sternness of thy tone and look:
Thine eye hath grown so clear, and bright, and dark,
Its thrilling glance mine own can hardly brook.
Speak not thus, sister; Sybil's love is true,
And there are others of strong faith, and sure;
For 'mid the false of earth, a very few
Still keep their trust holy, and high, and pure."

"There may be yet a few, and may it be
Thy blessed fate to meet them in thy life;
But *I* reck not for any, for to me
All life is weariness—all passion strife.
Yet place thy hand upon my heart and feel
How wildly rushes life's impatient tide;
But let it chafe! it has no power to steal
The strength away of a yet mightier pride.

"Sybil, thy years are few, and mine are so,
Yet have I learned what yet you have not known,
And I pray God that you may never know;
But thou didst catch the low, half-smothered moan,
Breathed by a spirit weary of its chains—
Pining in bondage of a scornful will,
That will not listen to its sad complains,
But sternly chides, and bids its voice be still."

"O Miriam, Miriam! has the withering blight
Of some chill frost fell on thy heart's sweet flowers,
Freezing the dew-drop that so pure and bright
Nurtured their bloom in thy life's sunny hours?

Has some false hand dared thy rich hopes to crush,
  And made the sunlight of thy dreaming dim?
Then every sob of grief and sorrow hush—
  Sybil could feel but scorn for such as him."

Ay, scorn for him—but would this make thee love
  Thy blighted life the more, that thy proud heart
Found refuge in disdain? It would but prove
  How deep the wound, how fell the laden dart.
But no, I mourn not for the love of one,
  But for the shadows of distrust that cling
To every show of virtue, till the sun
  Of life's sweet hope is darkened by its wing."

"But is it just or generous thus to think
  The world is naught but frailty and deceit,
Because one hand hath rudely broke the link
  That bound thy love to him in fetters sweet?
My gentle sister, *thou* should be too true
  To let distrust darken thy sunny way;
For still some hand around thy feet will strew
  Such flowers of love as fade not in a day."

"'Tis well thou thinkest gently of the world,
  But talk no more of its weak faith to me;
My heart's sweet dream is broken—ever furled
  My spirit's drooping pinion; and to be
A skeptic of earth's earnestness and truth
  Even hath a bitter pleasure; though so stern
It seems to thee that the full heart of youth
  Hath laid its treasures in love's crumbling urn."

"Miriam, my sister, bitterly I grieve
  That thou shouldst throw life's purest gems aside,
And smile in very mockery to give
  Their richness at the shrine of chilling pride.

O it is better that our faith and love
   A thousand times were trampled in the dust,
Than with such calm, cold, throbless hearts to move
   Through the fair earth alone—no hope—no trust."

THE MIDNIGHT BANNER.

Once upon a night of sorrow,
Sat I waiting for the morrow,
With my hand upon my forehead,
   And a grief upon my heart;
One I loved had rashly spoken
Words by which our hearts are broken—
Fatal words, of bitter meaning,
   Such as force our souls apart;
And I sat in tearless sorrow
   Till the midnight should depart.

Then, to cool the fever burning
Like a flame my forehead, turning
To the closely-curtained window,
   I had drawn the folds aside;
When I saw, all bathed in moonlight,
Floating in the face of midnight,
Like a robed and winged spirit,
   A dark banner, long and wide,
Streaming out upon the night-wind
   In its lone and solemn pride.

With a motion slow and even,
Up against the starry heaven,
Floated that mysterious banner;
   Like a proud and mournful soul,

Brooding o'er a sorrow hidden
In a heart-cell, which, unbidden,
Human eye may ne'er discover—
  Human love may not console;
Sadly and in silence mourning
  Fate which nothing can control.

Like a disembodied spirit,
The wan moon was hovering near it,
With a face all dim and pallid,
  Just above the banner's height;
While it kept its murmuring motion,
Like a wave upon the ocean,
Or a sigh within a bosom
  Struggling back from human sight;
Heedless of the spirit shedding
  Round it her caressing light.

Long I gazed, almost forgetting
My own grieving and regretting,
On that dark, mysterious banner,
  Floating on the midnight wind;
And I borrowed from its seeming
Thoughts in that strange hour of dreaming,
That have left undying tokens
  Of themselves upon my mind;
And my spirit gathered from them
  Knowledge holy and refined.

All the wildness of my madness
Altered to a calmer sadness—
Under that dim banner marshaled,
  Memory viewed her countless host;
And my soul looked on confessing,
With a murmured prayer and blessing,
Each endearing reminiscence
  In the tide of passion lost;
And a thrill of hope and gladness
  My tumultuous bosom crossed.

Then the banner, like my spirit,
Ceased to waver, and more near it
Rode the pale moon, slow descending
  To the chambers of the west;
And then for one blissful minute,
The dark banner held within it
The pale spirit's lovely vision,
  Like a face within a breast;
And I knew by that sweet omen
  I should be forgiven and blessed.

THE COUNTRY ROAD.

I LOVE to muse along the tracery
Of a provincial road. The gaudy town,
With its full streets, its busy, care-browed throng,
May furnish food, ay, ample food for thought;
But such reflections as come o'er us there
Are feverish and unhealthy. But to me
There is sweet company in the old trees
That fling their shadows o'er the sunny way;
Whose murmur of innumerable leaves,
Broken by bursts of joyous harmony,
From the gay, bright-plumed choir, or by the quick,
Low, musical chattering of the small,
And many habitants of the old wood—
To find a flower, that half-concealed by leaves,
Had bloomed unseen (so many flowers of life
Are passed unheeded by, and careless feet
Trample them in the dust); all these have tongues,
That murmur in soft discourse to the heart.
The very shadows on the dusty way,
Changeful and restless, mock the swinging boughs

That suit their motion to the fitful breeze,
And whisper music to the dream-bound soul.
But most of all, I love to notice where
The feet of other wayfarers have fallen.
Such is the willingness with which we look
Into the hearts of others, to find out
The secret of their misery or bliss;
That as I gaze upon the brief impress
Of feet whose owners I have never known,
A shadow of their character will cross
The vision of my fancy like a truth.
Deep in the dust, and almost half erased,
I see the traces of a ponderous shoe;
The wearer hath trod heavily; perhaps
Burdened with care, as wearied with the toil
Of tedious miles; for when the heart beats low
The blood flows but reluctantly, and life
Performs its functions wearily, with care.
But here, and here, a little unshod foot
Hath pressed but lightly, as with smiling eyes
And bounding heart its infant owner tripped
Laughing along, perchance to school and books—
May be to gather flowers for good grandma—
Or yet to roam in search of winter stores
Of brown, delicious nuts.
                    And here's a print
Of a small slippered foot, and just beside
A larger and a heavier impress.
And now the mind with fancy's pencil draws
A picture of a pair, a beautiful pair,
Of young and love-eyed beings, who, with lips
Lovely and eloquent, breathe impassioned dreams,
Fashioned in hearts filled with the loveliest
And gentlest thoughts, and told in whispered words
Inspired by scenes as full of love as is
The countenance of Nature. They have talked,
Confiding in each other, till the chain
Of subtlest sympathy that binds our hearts

Hath linked theirs in blest unison, and made
Life seem a fairy-land of light and love.
But they are gone! I now no longer see
The tracery of their footsteps; but I go
Still dreaming on; and I will have a world
Of beautiful images; and some, perhaps,
Sad, sad ones, too; but these will make the heart
More grateful for its joys, and give a shade
To the too brilliant coloring of its dreams.

SONG OF THE EAGLE.

I'M the child of light, yet the darkest night
No terrors hath for me,
For the storm I ride, in a monarch's pride,
Or skim o'er the heaving sea.
When lowering clouds, like sable shrouds,
Wrap the earth in deepest gloom,
I join the surge in the funeral dirge,
O'er the sailor's watery tomb.

And I love to rest on the summit crest
Of the proudest mountain's height,
While the clouds below lie like wreaths of snow,
Yielding homage to my might.
In my pride I go where eternal snow
Has crested the mountain's brow,
And laugh at the storm, and the blackened form
Of the threatening clouds below.

Mid the lightning's flash, and the thunder's crash,
I scream for my own delight,
For I love to hear, so loud and clear,
My voice ringing out in the night.

Not so proud a one ever gazed on the sun
As the eagle bird, I trow,
Stooping to rest on the towering crest
Of the highest mountain's brow.

In the pride of a king, with folded wing,
I gaze on ruined Tyre;
By Heaven's decree it was given to me,
And no power to give is higher.
From land or sea God hath chosen me,
And a favored bird am I—
The gifted of Heaven, to whom power is given
Over earth, and sea, and sky.

I care not for earth, though I had my birth
On the proudest height she owns;
And I'd rather ride o'er old ocean's tide
Than sit on her rocky thrones.
But I love the sun, and could I have won
A home in its realms of light,
With a laugh of scorn from this earth I'd turn,
And soar to my home in delight.

AUTUMN.

Autumn breezes now are blowing,
Groves with rainbow colors glowing,
Flowers dim and faded growing,
Fading with the year!
Louder sounds the rushing river,
More the forest leaves do quiver,
Through the boughs the wild winds shiver,
With a voice of fear.

Wildly sweet is its low moaning,
Our sad hearts with rapture toning,
Every chord its power owning,
Yielding a soft thrill;
Clouds across the sky are straying
Leaves in whirling eddies playing,
Birds their farewell notes essaying,
Making concert shrill.

Spirits through the earth are gliding,
In the forest shadows hiding,
Mourning for the short abiding
Of earth's witching bloom:
Hear them when the daylight endeth,
When the dusky eve descendeth,
And her sable pinion blendeth
All things into gloom.

Heed them when the clouds are flying,
In low, solemn whispers sighing,
From each little nook replying,
With a wail of fear:
List them where the insect hummeth,
Where the misty sunlight cometh,
Where the tiny cascade foameth,
Making music clear.

Roam by wood, or field, or river,
Everywhere their voices quiver,
With a sweet, low cadence ever,
Mourning beauty's doom!
Silence now more silent seemeth,
Each bright planet brighter beameth,
And the young moon colder gleameth
Through the solemn gloom.

Now do I go forth communing,
My wild spirit rapture owning,

Thrilling to the whispered moaning
Of the spirit choir;
Fountains in my heart upgushing,
Dim remembrance o'er.me rushing,
Eye and cheek most brightly flushing
With a welcome fire.

Did each season bring such gladness,
Rapture so mixed up with sadness,
Soon would a delicious madness
Steal my heart away:
Every leaf with crimson gleaming,
Is with pensive fancies teeming,
Bringing dim, unconscious dreaming,
Bright and brief as they.

THE DYING POET.

He knew that he was dying; day by day
He felt the silver chords within his bosom
Mysteriously but palpably give way,
And he cared not that death so soon should loose them;
For a dull grief was carking in his breast,
That while his heart beat would not be at rest.

There had been flowers in his course at morn,
But one by one had withered on his way;
His heart was heavy, and his feet were torn,
And yet no close came to his weary day;
The night was distant, but he prayed to die
Before its shadows darkened in his sky.

Many had blessed him as he passed them by,
And hushed their hearts to listen to his singing;
And shouted his name upward to the sky—
Roses and gems upon his pathway flinging;
But fainting he had turned him from the throng,
Sighing his sorrow to himself and song.

There had been one to whom his heart went forth
In his young manhood—love's free gift, unbidden;
But she was fair and frigid as the north,
And the warm breathings of his lyre were chidden:
And from that hour it took an altered tone,
Singing to Nature and itself alone.

But now his course was ended; and his gaze
Watched the red sunset fading from the sky—
The last his eyes might look on; while a maze
Of half-forgotten memories flitted by;
A breeze came from the sea and stirred his hair,
And fancy felt his mother's fingers there.

Deeper the crimson of the sunset grew;
An old church-tower that loomed against the west,
Lifting its pinnacle to the far blue,
Pictured to him his own deserted breast,
That rent and ruined, let the sunset in,
Gilding in mockery the shapeless scene.

How had his life been wasted; he had spent
His youth, his manhood, all his young bright years,
In giving one poor passion its full vent,
And it rewarded him with heart-wrung tears,
Till the slow fever sapped his veins all dry,
Nor blood refreshed his heart, nor tears his eye.

Then like an old man with a century's weight
Bowing him to the dust, he laid his weary head

Upon the arm of death, and waiting sat,
Wishing the moments of probation fled—
Wishing his sun of life would fade away,
With the departing brightness of the day.

And thus was hushed his heart, and hushed his lyre;
Death had o'ercome him with the twilight's shade;
The altar had consumed with its own fire,
And perished with the gift upon it laid;
The idol was an idol now no more—
The Poet's love, and grief, and song were o'er.

JUDAS' REMORSE.

Priests! take them back, those thirty blood-stained pieces!
For which I sold what worlds can not redeem;
With every pulse my fearful sin increases,
And my brain throbs as in some fevered dream.
"See thou to that!" ay, ye do well to taunt
The cursed instrument of your own crime—
Fiends! take your bribe—away with it, avaunt!
Give me a respite, one small hour of time.

I will go forth to look upon the earth,
Upon whose face I am so foul a stain,
And will return no more, for from my birth
If I have lived for this, how worse than vain!
Now on the temple's pinnacle I stand,
And my eye scans the motley gaping crowd,
Whose murderous deed shall lay this fated land,
Accursed and blackened, in a bloody shroud.

The Master's words—oh, how they haunt me now!
  And burn like coals of vengeance on my heart;
And the word "traitor," branded on my brow,
  From which I never, never more can part!
Oh, that I ne'er had seen Him, had ne'er heard
  Those heavenly accents from His guileless lips;
Like hissing firebrands, in my brain each word
  Quenches itself, and of my life-blood sips.

I knew, I knew such words and deeds belonged
  But to the Deity, and to Him alone!
But powers of darkness all around me thronged
  And longed to claim me, as I am, their own.
Oh, would I were the lowliest thing that lives,
  Even a soulless, a just breathing thing!
For what is intellect, that to us gives
  Such power to sin, such fearful suffering brings?

I dare not ask for pardon; He hath said
  Wo to the traitor! and His word fails not;
What if I die? When He shall wake the dead,
  Then shall I find I have not been forgot.
They lead Him forth! Oh, agonizing sight!
  On His meek head a rugged crown of thorns;
But were it gold His brow would dim its light,
  Such the pure majesty these wretches scorn.

The royal robe in mockery He wears;
  They spit upon Him, and they hail Him king!
And now, O God! His heavy cross He bears,
  Nor breathes one word for all His suffering.
Why do I live—oh, why behold this scene,
  Whose shade will haunt me through eternity?
Off, coward fears! your slave too long I've been,
  But now I am resolved, and I *will die!*

THOUGHTS OF THEE.

As the wild-bird, when the spring-flower
Cometh back once more,
Seeketh the same greenwood bower
It had loved before;
So my memory never loseth
Its sad dream of thee;
But my heart around it closeth,
Fondly, mournfully.

It doth bide with me forever,
Waking or asleep—
Murmuring like some mournful river,
Low, and wild, and deep.
Every thing that's good and lovely,
All fair things I see,
Do like hidden music move me,
With sad dreams of thee.

Summer clouds are beautiful,
And sunny spots in groves;
And the gushing of a waterfall
Hath a melting voice like love's;
And the young moon hath a witchery
No tongue hath ever told,
As she looketh down in purity,
So bright, and fair, and cold.

But my heart forgets its dreaminess,
Its once so frequent thrill;
And gazeth upon loveliness
With pulses strangely still.
I can not tear myself away,
I can not break the spell;
But it doth strengthen day by day,
Repulse it as I will.

For there was not the smallest thing
    That was admired by thee,
To which my spirit does not cling
    Watchfully, tenderly.
I sit beneath the evening sky,
    And look upon the moon,
And the fitful breeze comes flutt'ring by,
    With a low and hollow tune;

And I see our beacon star come up,
    And rise above the trees,
And the dew is in the Iris' cup,
    But what to me are these?
I know *thou* wilt not come again,
    As was thy wont of old;
And I press my burning brow in pain,
    And wish the night were told:

For the moonlight teems with memory,
    And the stars burn on my sight;
And every thing doth talk of thee,
    In the stillness of the night.
In dreams I sometimes see thy face,
    But nothing kind is there;
I meet thy mute, forgetful gaze,
    With still but deep despair.

The sunlight is too bright for me,
    And pleasant days seem long;
Laughter is but a mockery,
    And the voice of happy song.
I do not weep, but crush my heart,
    That I may seem to be
Unwounded by the poison dart
    That was prepared for me.

My spirit walks the earth apart,
    Weary and alone,

And not a chord in all my heart,
    But hath a broken tone.
The chords that once so wildly rung
    To mirth and melody,
Are silent now, or only strung
    To mournful thoughts of thee

THE GRAVE OF L. E. L.

"Not where the wild bee hummeth
  About the mossed headstone;
And at midnight the moon cometh
  And looketh down alone."

Thy grave is not befitting one like thee,
  Sweet but impassioned songstress of the heart;
They should have laid thee 'neath some spreading tree,
  From all but wild-wood melodies apart.
They should have laid thee by some low-voiced river,
  Whose waves would keep for thee a soft complain,
Murmuring with plaintive, dirge-like voice, forever
  To thy calm rest a wild, pathetic strain.

The clang of armor never should have rung
  Above the mouldering dust of one like thee;
Thou couldst not love the trumpet's brazen tongue,
  Who didst find life such bitter mockery;
And it was mockery to lay thee there,
  Beneath an Eastern pavement's burning glow,
With heavy tread of soldiers falling where
  The sacred tear of memory should flow.

Was there no one whose delicate sympathy
  Could choose for thee a holier place of rest,
And o'er the heart once rich with harmony,
  See that the earth and the young wild-flowers prest?

We may now chide the soldier's iron heel
  That stamps relentlessly upon thy grave;
But ah, thy living heart did often feel
  More heavy griefs from which we could not save.

And thou, whose theme was ever passionate love,
  Whose lyre e'er sounded with a sad complain
Of unrequited sympathies, that wove
  Thy dearest happiness with thy deepest pain,
Art sleeping now where not a flower may spring,
A leaf may quiver, or a wild bird sing.

FOREBODING.

More and more by daily sorrow
  Is the bright veil drawn aside,
That was wont the sad to-morrow
  From the fair to-day to hide.

More and more with wild emotion
  Is my spirit tossed and torn;
While upon life's troubled ocean
  Fearful, shadowy shapes are borne.

In the future's dim uncertain,
  Gathering clouds obscure the light,
Hanging like a sable curtain
  Over all that once was bright.

Murmurs in my soul keep sighing
  Like the tempest's rising tone,
Into solemn silence dying,
  With a low bewailing moan.

Shall this scathing tempest find me?
  Is this shadow but a shade?
Pain, and fear, and darkness blind me,
  And my spirit shrinks afraid.

Backward have I looked imploring,
  But the sky is overcast;
And the clouds of doubt are lowering
  Even oe'r the sunny past.

How hath sorrow bruised my spirit,
  Clouded all my hopes and dreams,
Till no light of gladness near it
  Shines upon its troubled streams.

Where hath fled the glorious vision
  That enchained my soul so long;
Points it now in stern derision
  To my faded flowers of song?

Is there then no resurrection
  Of the spirit's buried strength?
Penance done, and sad reflection,
  Will restore the boon at length.

Gloom and sorrow I will banish,
  Tempests *shall* be overcome;
Phantom fears shall all evanish,
  Exiled to their proper tomb.

If my spirit faint or falter,
  Glorious vision, lend thine aid!
Thou shalt shine above the altar
  Where my hope and trust are laid.

MY LOVE.

Love thee? I must! not the great sea
Ever heaves upward to the moon
As my soul lifts itself to thee,
Drawn by the magic of thine own.
My heart is like a fountain springing
In shadow of some lonely tree,
Its constant streams and ceaseless singing,
Murmur and flow alone to thee.

I would I did not love thee so,
Lest God should desolate the shrine,
And lay the glorious image low
So like to His, so like to thine!
And could I deem the light that now
Halos h y being would depart,
I would unsay my holy vow,
Though it in breaking broke my heart.

But thou, thou never sure canst be
Less of a glory than this hour,
And my soul rests relyingly
On thine, as on a nobler power.
Day's glorious morn, her holy eve,
The grand, the beautiful, the bright,
Each in the soul's existence weave
New thoughts of thee like rays of light.

Such love as this will burn till life
Has darkened in its narrow cell,
And calmly 'mid the world's fierce strife,
As sheltered in some fairy dell.
I only ask that thou wilt be
What now thou art, for evermore,
Peerless, yet bright'ning constantly,
As soul refining leaves its ore.

HEART-BREATHINGS.

And must we thus bear on, thus give to pride
A mastery not its own; wear a bright brow
Wreathed with cold smiles that come not from the heart,
And clothe our thoughts in language of the mind,
While the soul lies a writhing, moaning thing,
Beneath this calm exterior? Oh! must
A thousand gushing impulses be crushed,
Ground by the heel of pride, that lifts its brow
With a false garnish—as the ivy gives
Freshness to what is fallen in decay,
While the heart perishes?
O for the privilege which the world grants not,
To be but what we are! True, there may pass
Over our hearts a devastating fire,
A scorching blast to lay them desolate;
But from the ashes of the past may spring
A stronger blossom, with a deeper glow,
"Than tinged its earliest flower."

The glancing streams,
That play through all our hearts impulsively,
May find a deep, broad channel, where their flow,
Thenceforward will be silent, low, and strong;
But oh, must it be hidden? Then give back
The storm and lightning—let the tempest howl—
It were far easier than this, to bear
The constant wearing of the heart away!

THE DEAD LOVER.

Is he then dead, O God! and hath he perished
 In all his brightness—stricken back to dust!
The high imaginings—the hopes he cherished—
 And my mad love—alike an empty trust?
It can not, can not be; look on his brow!
 The light of intellect is resting there;
And the calm smile upon his proud lip now,
 Hath the same sweetness it was wont to wear.

Oft have I gazed upon his manly face,
 And felt my heart throb with a lofty pride
To mark the same expression I now trace,
 Of high, pure thoughtfulness; the soul's full tide
Of still but mighty feelings shining through
 Each soul-illumined feature; would not *Death*,
With his damp, icy touch, and blighting dew,
 Efface the impress with his first cold breath?

Yet say they, "He is dead!" I may now dare
 To lay my hand upon his kingly brow,
And smooth the masses of his jetty hair,
 Whose glossy curls have never until now
Threaded my trembling fingers; strange delight!
 How my heart burns within its prisoning cell!
And my brain reels, till all around is night—
 Would 'twere death's silent and insidious spell!

The brief insensibility is past;
 And deeper than before the rankling dart
Pierces its barbed point; oh, shall this last,
 And life yet linger in this heaving heart?

Away, away! come ye to tear me hence?
  If in his life I dared not tell my love,
Awed into silence by his eloquence,
  Leave me alone with him, that I may prove

By my wild grief, how wild, and strong, and deep
  Was the revering love I bore for him;
My aching eyes, that burn too much to weep,
  With unshed tears must be forever dim;
And this rent heart, torn from its lofty trust,
  Must, sad and strengthless, sink again to earth,
And, like its idol, mingle with the dust,
  From which it rose in its mysterious birth.

O for a single tone of his deep voice,
  To linger ever quivering on my ear!
O for one glance of those dark, earnest eyes
  To light the gloom of this now joyless sphere!
But thou art still and silent—thou art dead!
  I feel what death is now—voiceless and still;
When the bright spirit from the clay is fled—
  And thou art thus—motionless, voiceless, chill!

And we were to be wedded—I thy bride;
  And I am thine still, even in the tomb;
Though never more triumphant by thy side,
  I feel to my hot cheek the quick blood come.
I know our souls are wedded—but to see
  Thy face forever hidden from my sight—
Never to hear thy voice—oh, agony!
  Would that my spirit, too, might wing its flight.

TO ——.

Had I not known all that the heart can tell
  Of bliss or sorrow, ere *thy* love was told,
My heart had broken at thy last farewell—
  Proud, tender, thrilling, yet that seemed so cold.
But sad regret was all that I could give—
  Regret, that all that might have been my own
My heart rejected loathingly, to live
  In its mute passion, grieving and alone;
And a sharp sorrow for the pang I gave,
Though it had been thy "double death" to save.

'Twas no new tale that thy lips whispered me;
  It is the curse of genius thus to steal
The hearts of many after it, yet be
  Lonely and longing ever; and to feel
That though 'tis love we want, the love we win
  Is a poor, earthly sense, to which the dream
We cherish is a heavenly; and the sin
  Of hollow-heartedness is made to seem
Ours, and a strange ingratitude, while we
Crush in our full hearts our hushed misery.

Yet not thus *thou:* there was a nobleness
  That won me unto thee as friend to friend;
And though I could not suffer thy caress,
  Nor to thy love a joyful listening lend,
It was a joy sometimes to hear thy tone,
  In its full depth more eloquent than song,
Blend with the spell of poesy its own,
  And in its soothing cadence flow along,
While my heart stole the music of the rhyme,
And beat harmoniously with the sweet chime.

Thy praise was pleasant and thy kindness dear,
 And all was won that can be given, but love;
And that was a closed fountain; not a tear,
 Of all its old-time fullness would there move
To the wild breath of passion! all was still.
 The calm but mocked the tumult in thy soul,
And Hope's death brought the agonies that kill;
 While all thy manhood struggled for control,
My heart was writhing in its bitterness,
That it could not be loved, and yet loved less.

And for this we are parted. Each has lost
 Something they prized the highest; and both feel
As if their path of fortune had been crossed:
 Thou with thy wound too rankling soon to heal,
And me with my sad heart made still more sad;
 But in the hearts of both is a consoling grief,
A mournfulness more sweet than being glad,
 That could not find in pleasure a relief;
Yet would I lose my memory of thee,
To know thy burdened spirit once more free.

LOVE.

I CAN not love the happy: those who seem
Never to have known sorrow, from whose hearts
Gushes continually the caroling
Of thoughtless pleasure; unless it be the joy—
The glad and innocent mirth of children—
Bursting in happiness from out pure hearts
Fresh from the hand of Deity. But man,
Who has seen life, beheld its miseries,
Whose thoughts have reached the compass of ripe years,

Should have within his heart a ceaseless spring
Of gentle and out-welling sympathies;
And they should course throughout his spirit's being,
As mountain rivulets traverse the earth—
Refreshing in their course each drooping flower—
Renewing beauty in each withered plant—
And helping everywhere to germinate
The seeds of virtue.

And thus would mirth be chaste, and life be joy,
And all our wild propensities be checked;
And all our eagerness for gaudy show,
That so contrasts with pale-cheeked suffering,
Would die. This would be real happiness!
And those whom purity makes sensitive
Would shrink no more, but ivy-like entwine
The tendrils of affection round strong hearts.
Love is a byword—friendship but a name—
And though we use them, rarely do we think
How strong, and deep, and thrilling is their power!
"God is love!" it is His very essence;
And yet the spirit of the Godhead man
Treats mockingly, and makes a jest of all
The gentler and the purer attributes
Of soul! O that the spirit of true love,
Untrammeled, unrestrained, might wander forth,
Breathing a balm on every bleeding heart—
Binding up wounds—forgiving injury—
And by uniting each dissevered link,
Encircle the great family of man
In one electric chain of sympathy!
Then would our earth again be Paradise,
And man, though heir to suffering, yet soothed
By gentleness and love, would be more chaste—
Like gold tried by refiners—and more fit
To win his great inheritance of love,
And life eternal!

NIGHT WHISPERS.

O WHAT a night is this! The glorious stars
With their sweet, solemn gaze, seeming to look
Into our very souls. Gently! it mars
The lovely dream if even a word be spoke,
That comes not like soft music to the ear,
Murmured, and low, and making harmony
With the still music of that higher sphere—
So let no discord break the melody.

This is the hour for soul-communion meet;
For talking of dear loves and holy things;
Of themes that to the spirit are most sweet,
And for the full heart's sweet unburdenings.
I can almost imagine that my heart
Hath grown too holy for a sinful thought;
So much the gentle images that start
From past and present with this hour are fraught.

The past hath memories of the dear dreams
Of early years—of longings after love—
Something to fill the heart, to drink its streams
Of pure and earnest tenderness—inwove
With visions of the future, which were blent
Of hope and trust, the trust of our first years,
Which ne'er returns when once it hath been lent
To a false faith, to be dissolved in tears.

That glowing dream is not yet wholly fled,
But its fair hues have taken a deeper dye;
As the pale light the twilight stars have shed,
Is deepened to full radiance in the sky.

The heart still sadly longeth, and in vain;
For earth is insufficient to its love,
And many a wild and startling thrill of pain,
Its too keen sensitiveness still doth prove.

But there is such a joy, a joy so sweet—
So pure a transport in an hour like this—
When heart from heart an answering throb may meet,
In union to which silence adds a bliss;
When the soft clasp of a caressing hand,
Or the clear glance of an expressive eye,
Can make the mutual spirit understand
All the fine thoughts that in its depths may lie.

Our pleasures are so sweet that we forget
That we have grieved for suffering or sin,
And only feel a sad and soft regret
That all is not forever thus within.
O night! thy solemn beauty fills my soul
With a deep rapture, not unlike to prayer;
Delicious joy, which I would not control,
And only to be perfect need to share.

If there are hours when the soul receives
On its unwritten pages worlds of thought,
Methinks that now some spirit's spotless leaves
Full many a bright imagining hath caught;
And many a note of song, the voiceless song
Of the soul, mingled with the viewless choir
Thrilling all nature, and whose tones belong
To the great Source that nature doth inspire.

SMILES.

Have you ne'er felt, when the laugh rang out
With the merry peal and the echoed shout,
And the jest flew round with a hearty glee,
And the bright eye laughed right merrily—
Have you ne'er felt that the shaft of pain
Was meant to be clothed in that merry strain?

And did not the thought, like a magic spell,
Choke up your voice with your spirit's swell,
And your tone grow hoarse while you laughed on still,
Though it fell on your heart with a painful thrill;
And you trembled and shrunk like a guilty thing,
Lest the tears should escape their hidden spring?

And a word, a single careless word,
Fell from the lips that many heard;
But you of the hearers alone knew well
What that careless word was meant to tell;
Still you jested on with a hearty glee,
Though your heart sunk cold and joylessly!

And there was an eye you feared to meet,
Lest its glance should sink to the deep retreat
Of the burning thoughts and scalding tears
That sear the heart with grief of years,
And awaken the fountain that must o'erflow,
Lest it burst the heart with its strength of woe!

Far down in the spirit's deep, deep well,
There was hidden a grief that none might tell;
For the eye laughed on, and the lip was bright,
And none might dream of hopeless night
Whose shadow so heavy and cheerless all,
Had wrapt your heart in its gloomy pall.

O trust not smiles, for their light may hide
A heart where each gushing hope hath died;
And guide your lips, lest the careless jest
Should sadden a heart that hath long supprest
Its harrowing fears with a careless air,
And bound with a smile-wreath the brow of despair.

TO A BEAUTIFUL COQUETTE.

Say on; if I but hear thy lips
  Make music with their balmy breath,
It is enough! I do not ask
  That they revoke their doom of death.

Yes, I did take the poisoned cup
  From thy fair hand, and madly drink;
And now, when I have found 'tis death,
  Now, even now, I do not shrink.

Speak! tell me that my fevered brain
  Was phrensied when I've thought thou'st smiled;
That the sweet hope I nursed so long
  Was ill-begotten—Fancy's child.

Call me thy slave—a fond, mad fool—
  Thou'lt say, alas, one mournful truth,
For I have wasted in this dream
  The best of life, the pride of youth.

Say this, and more, and with the scorn
  That suits thee better than thy smile,
Thy frown, though bitter, can not harm—
  'Tis in the sweetness lurks the guile!

Ay, let thy proud lip wear for me
  The scornful curve it graces so;
The challenge may perchance call forth
  My slumbering pride—I do not know.

Yet hardly still can I despise
  The falsehood that hath been so sweet;
Hardly, when thinking on our past,
  My burning words of scorn repeat.

Yet do I scorn thee ; in my soul
  My nobler nature spurns thy art;
And though my senses are enthralled,
  A higher shrine must have my heart.

Go, fair enchantress; not thy brow,
  Or lip, or cheek, or witching grace,
Or *seeming* worth, can ever win
  In this changed heart a lasting place.

SNOWDROPS.

O TAKE away your snowdrops pale, I can not bear the sight—
They were woven in our Ada's hair upon her bridal night;
And fairer looked the snowy buds than India's rarest pearls,
And fairer than them both the brow that beamed beneath her curls.
That lily brow, those tresses dark, O ne'er so fair a bride
Hath trembled at the altar-place her chosen one beside;
And never heart more pure and fond, a wedding gift was brought
Than Ada's in its sinlessness, its sweet and earnest thought.
The snowy robe, and lily brow, and bridal garland pale,
And dark bright tresses shining through the silver-woven vail;

The delicately tinted cheek, the bright lips' sweet unrest,
That quivered all unconsciously to the pulse within her breast;
The drooping eyelid glittering with bright and happy tears—
The memory of that bridal night hath haunted me for years.

But take away your pale, pale wreath, I can not bear the sight;
I saw it on our Ada's brow upon another night;
Another night—O if her brow outshone the wreath before,
Sure nothing earthly matched the white her brow and cheek then wore:
So pallid that the tracery of the blue, delicate vein
Upon the temple passed away, with all its violet stain;
Gone was all light, all radiance; with moveless lip and limb
She listened to the dreadful words they whispered her of him;
The husband of her bridehood false! her frightened soul seemed flown,
And the pale buds to wreathe a brow above a heart of stone.
O beautiful, most beautiful, but like a marble vase,
Whence life and perfume both are fled, the beauty of her face;
For fearfully and fatally the sudden terror came,
And quenched her life as would the sea a little incense flame;
And standing like a Hindoo girl who sees her lamp expire,
Her soul died out as music dies along a breaking lyre.
That night the wreath that decked the bride was loosened from her hair,
And the dark tresses straitened back with still and reverent care.

But soon again we wove a wreath of buds as white as snow;
We could not bear that even the grave should witness to her woe;
We twined them with her braided hair, and placed them on her breast,
And laid her softly down to sleep in a sweet place of rest;
But these fair buds bring back the scene, and the two that went before,
Then bring to twine about my brow your snowy wreath no more;
For fairer though they be than pearls, I can not bear the sight
Of snowdrops woven in a wreath since that remembered night.

BIRTHDAY OF AUTUMN.

Early awake this morn! my spirit shook
  Drowsiness from its plumes before the birds;
And up beside my window with a book,
  I strive to find a magic in the words.
But thought claims precedence; and with my eye
  Playing to lore the truant, I look on
Village and field, and river, wood and sky
  Just bright'ning with the first September sun.

Autumn has come again, the autumn-time
  Ever so glorious in our lovely land;
And where is there a lovelier? What clime
  Yields such a wealth of blessings to your hand?
But what I love in the autumnal days
  Is their delicious dreaminess, that fills
The spirit with a mellow, golden haze
  Like that throughout the atmosphere; one thrills,

If a leaf flutter on the wayside trees,
  Or insect sudden wind its tiny horn,
Or if springs up anon the fitful breeze,
  Scattering the leaves its idle force had torn.
There is a conscious bliss in every thing;
  The very shadows deeper, cooler seem,
Making us wish that we aside could fling
  Life's waking cares, and lay us down and dream.

The sun's rays grown less vertical, have now
  The soft gold that the painters imitate;
And tones come whispered from each waving bough,
  Sweeter than all that genius can create:

The low, wild, shivering music of the leaves,
That move like ripples on a silver sea,
Sinking and swelling ever, as it heaves
Soft wavering sighs of pensive melody.

When, too, the yellow-garbed October comes,
With breezy days, and grand, wild, moonlight nights;
When louder every busy insect hums
The requiem of its day so short and bright;
And when men love the sunshine, not the shade,
Sitting at noon beneath the leafless vine,
That in the summer dewy coolness made,
And bore the flowers that Beauty loved to twine.

Even the chill November throws sometimes
Aside her cloudy mantle, and looks out
With a warm azure sky, tempting the chimes
Of lingering birds and childhood's merry shout.
But must we close the window; we can lie
Snug in our easy chairs, and read or dream,
Musing how oft the seasons hurry by,
Leaving us ever farther down life's stream.

O if the autumn of our life came on
Prepared for winter like the fading year,
With plenty stored, and summer labor done,
There would be little in old age to fear.
Youth's feverish pulses would have grown more cold,
Its dark locks braided with some threads of gray;
But the wise heart, like wine that has grown old,
Gains without losing by the long delay.

THE HEART'S REQUIEM.

"A REQUIEM! and for whom?
For beauty in its bloom?
For valor fallen—a broken rose or sword?
A dirge for king or chief,
With pomp of stately grief,
Banner, and torch, and waving plume deplored?

"Not so! it is not so!"
No sounding wail of woe
Swells to the heavens when human hearts lie dead;
No torch lights up the gloom
Of the heart's rayless tomb;
No funeral incense o'er its dust is shed.

Wild was that heart's distress,
Fierce the dark bitterness
With which it bore its heavy griefs untold;
Scorning the poor relief
The false world offers grief—
Disdaining sympathy so false and cold.

Silent, unwept, alone
Breathing into the tone
Of its last long and passionate farewell,
Whole treasures of rich thought,
With the soul's fullness fraught,
Then dying with the melody's last swell.

Not the loud mournful dirge,
Sung by the ocean's surge,
Above the grave where buried thousands lie,
Rises to Heaven's high throne
With more emphatic tone,
Or with a note of purer majesty.

In one poor human heart
These thrilling accents start,
And mingle into music wild and deep;
Swelling in one rich strain
Of earthly joy and pain,
Then trembling softly, die away to sleep.

O for earth's hapless trust!
Its "mingled mind and dust"
Make with each other such continual strife!
O for the hapless faith
That meets reward in death,
Mourning the bitter chilliness of life.

Earth, earth! thy sods have pressed
Lightly on many a breast
That could not bear its weight of living woe;
Full many a heart hath come
To thy embrace of gloom,
Blessing thy coldness to the world's false glow.

"One more, then, one more strain
To earthly joy and pain,
A rich, and deep, and passionate farewell!
Pour out each fervent thought
With fear, hope, trembling fraught,
Into the notes the last this heart shall swell."

"MY SOUL IS DARK."

Ever down Time's rapid river,
Toward the distant, dim Forever,
Ceasing not, and ceasing never—
  From this mortal shore,
Is our life forever sliding,
Gliding still, and ever gliding,
With no pause, and no abiding,
  Till Time's tide is o'er.

I am sitting in the glimmer
Of the twilight growing dimmer,
As the stars begin to shimmer
  Through the darkening blue;
And my soul is sad to weeping,
With the memories 'tis keeping,
Memories that know no sleeping,
  No nepenthean dew.

Life's frail bark is onward drifting,
Where care's stormy winds are shifting,
And no cloud of darkness lifting
  Lets the light shine through;
Backward do I look with yearning,
My sad soul intensely burning,
But for me there is no turning—
  Onward I must go.

Onward borne, but backward looking,
While my anguished soul is brooking
All the gentle, sad rebuking
  Of the Past's dim face;
Forms from memory's shore entreating,
Beckon me unto their meeting,
But I can not—farther fleeting
  From each dear embrace.

Lo! the parting distance groweth,
And the river deeper floweth,
And the sky no signal showeth
    All is dark and drear;
Without oar or pilot floating—
Fearful is such lonely boating,
Where, unseen, the ear is noting
    Mighty depths a-near!

Hark! I hear the river's pouring,
Mingling with the ocean's roaring—
God! I lift to Thee imploring
    My benighted heart;
Be thou with me on life's river,
Guide me to the great Forever—
Light, and Help, and Glory ever,
    Thou my Pharos art!

A LETTER.

I LOOK upon the young moon in the sky,
And my thoughts image thee! Have you forgot
That which I told you in the sweet "lang syne,"
When I was young enough to dream of faith
Kept for a lifetime sacred? Hollow dream!
Ah, then I told you on a happy hour,
On a night like to this, that while the moon
Brightened and darkened to my living eyes,
There was one image should rise when it rose,
Shine as it shone, and should set darkly never!
That was my heart's first vow. My lips had breathed
Girlhood's "forget-me-not," and "ever-thine,"

To other ears before; but 'twas the strain
The wind awakens passing o'er a lyre—
The natural melody the young heart yields
Even to love's lightest whisper. But there came
At length a master, with the power to thrill
The finest chord in all the spirit's being.
Thou wert the master; and thy hand awoke
All of the slumbering music in my soul—
The strain whose echo lingers in my heart,
Resounding through its labyrinths forever.
But 'tis the echo *only* that remains;
The strain is still forever, and the chords
Of the soft lyre that thrilled so wildly then,
Would break in shrinking from the very touch
That once made such sweet singing. But 'tis past.
I have been sad and happy many times
Since we together have e'er wept or smiled;
And my heart beats as ever was its wont—
Slowly and pensively—save now and then,
When the desire for love grows suddenly strong,
And all the slumbering lava of the heart
Pours itself through the channels of the blood,
Making thought feverish, and the pulses high.
But this was in my nature, and 'twas this
Pining for love, and pride of intellect,
That made thee seem so godlike in my eyes.
But thou of all thy glory hast been shorn,
And thy great gifts are nothing to the shame
Of the mean sin of falsehood. I forget
The selfish thought that thy deceit wronged me,
In sorrow for the ruin that was wrought
In the most perfect beauty of the soul,
When the vail parted, and I saw untruth
Wedded to bright-browed wisdom.

Let it pass!
Or I shall make a lecture, which I meant not,
For I began by talking of the moon.

Ay, let it pass—it is a lesson more;
And daily we learn something of the world
Which it is well to know, though learning it
We tread on thorns where we saw only roses,
And find an ignis fatuus in a star.

A SCRAP FROM MY PORTFOLIO.

Nay, uncurl thy lip of pride,
  Scorn not wholly human weakness;
Thou shalt learn, when thou art tried,
  More of sin-forgiving meekness.

Is the world's condemning sneer
  Cast upon thy fellow-man?
Bravely let thy smile, thy tear,
  Cheer to virtue if it can.

Does the frail one pass thee by
  With a bended brow of sadness—
Frown not, in that heart *now* lie
  Thoughts that scorch the brain to madness.

Life is strong, and hearts are frail—
  In the struggle man may fall;
But if aught from us avail,
  Shall we answer not the call?

Check thy spirit's wayward scorn,
  Wreathe thy lip with smiles of love,
Bind the heart remorse hath torn,
  And let kindness virtue move.

Feel no shame that thou hast been
   Gentle to the erring one,
That the soul once dark with sin
   Fairer 'neath thy smile hath grown.

TO ONE WHO BADE ME "GO WIN A NAME."

Poet! whose prophetic numbers
   Seem to point me to a name,
Know that in my bosom slumbers
   Every pulse that wakes to fame.

Themes like mine are not for glory!
   Thoughts like mine win feeble praise;
Mine is not the classic story,
   Mine are not scholastic lays.

Not from tome of art or learning
   Came the spark of sacred fire;
But the *heart* within me burning,
   Formed itself into a lyre.

And among its frail shreds ever
   Spirit-voices whisper low—
Spirit-voices which are never
   Echoed in this world below.

Mind may be renowned for ages,
   Reason rear her altar high,
But the heart's more humble pages
   Live unread, and darkened die.

Like Eolian harp-chords waking
To each starting of the gale,
And in some strong tempest breaking
With a wild and mournful wail—

So the heart-strings thrill and quiver
To the world's rude borean breath,
Till the "silver cords" do sever,
Or are gently loosed by death.

So, as notes Eolian perish,
When the breeze has died away,
Will the soul-strains now I cherish
Live but only for a day.

MADELINE.

I NEVER saw aught like to what thou art—
A spirit so peculiar in its mould,
With so much wildness, and with yet a part
Of all the softer beauties we behold:
So dark and still at times, thy spirit seeming
Like waters sheltered from the shining sun,
Hidden in the dim mantle of its dreaming,
As if it joyed all earthliness to shun;

And yet again, emerging from its dream
Thy soul shines forth, pellucid as the air;
And O so lovely and so bright, we deem
That mortal sprite could never be so fair!
Thy thoughts in their rare current stilly gliding
Glimmer so starrily through thy pure eyes,
Revealing glimpses of the heart's wealth hiding
Within their depths, gem-bedded like the skies.

Thy form seems moulded in thy soul's own grace—
  Adapted to express each subtile thought—
So fair and lucid is thy lily face,
  Thy motion with such witchery is fraught.
There is so much in every act of thine,
  That tells thy soul keepeth an angel guard,
Their glorious wings do almost seem to shine
  A heavenly halo round their lovely ward.

Alas! when I do gaze on thee, my spirit
  Longeth for Paradise, and vaguely dreams,
Wondering if there itself will not inherit
  Some of such brightness as around thee beams:
Surely the music, and the unfading flowers,
  And forms of light that walk the courts of heaven,
Do fill thy visions in thy musing hours,
  So that to thee their semblance has been given.

TO EDITH MAY.

I HAVE not seen thee, Edith May; they say thy face is fair—
But I know thy soul, that is not seen, and know it high and rare;
And I love thee by a sign that's given to every poet soul—
That spirit-linking sympathy beyond our own control.
There is a lyre within my heart as there is one in thine,
But a plaintive, low-voiced, murmuring thing is this frail lyre of mine;
Not grand, and wild, and proudly toned, yet scorning mirth withal,
Like the harps our fancy hears at times in some old knightly hall;
But softly glad and wildly sad, with a thousand nameless strings
That wake, as doth the rose-leaf wake, to the breath of unseen things.

Not less for this it echoes all the tones of higher skill,
And trembles most with rapture when another's touch can thrill.
For this I love thee, Edith May, thy spirit's voice I hear,
Like the strain of some grand melody resounding in my ear;
And visions rise before my eyes of hosts in armor bound,
And like a voice within a dream, I hear the clarion's sound;
And gorgeous banners broidered o'er with many a strange design,
With burnished lance and waving plume, deck out the shadowy line—
Anon the sunset's crimson cloud is fading o'er the hill,
And the chieftain's farewell bugle-note is sounding sad and shrill;

And standing on the castle wall I see a lady fair,
With pallid face, and waving scarf, and unbound raven hair;
While winding up the distant hill the long defile hath passed,
And the lady on the chief she loved hath fondly looked her last.
All old-time scenes of war and pomp, of love and minstrelsy,
Of kingly sports, and courtly dames, and knightly rivalry;
All by-gone themes once wont to stir the blood of princely men,
Swell my dreaming heart with lofty pride, and the dead past lives again;
And I love thy harp's grand tone that wakes my spirit's high romance,
And praise thee that thou hast for thine this rich inheritance.

I have a sister, Edith May, a sister pure and young,
With a holy heart, and gifted mind, and sweetly eloquent tongue;
And to her I bear a feeling which can have no earthly name,
But our souls are linked, our hearts are joined, and our loves are aye the same;
And a glorious world of dreams have we, a rare poetic world,
Where fancy's restless golden wings are glittering unfurled—
Where love sits like a household form, a dear, familiar thing,
And countless fairy visions float forever on the wing;
And here amid the whispered strains of spirit-minstrelsy,
I listen with my dreaming soul for one wild note from thee.

I have not seen thee, Edith May—they call thy youthful face
The lovely index of the soul, its poetry and grace;

And blest I deem that thou must be, so gifted, young, and fair,
Yet these alone fill not the heart if love be wanting there;
For hearts like ours, dear Edith May, need love as do the flowers
The breath of the caressing wind and heaven's genial showers:
And I would breathe a prayer to God to bless thy heart's young
dream,
But with those peerless gifts of thine my prayer would idle seem.
Then fare-thee-well, young poetess! may not my waiting ear
List long in vain for that wild strain it loveth most to hear.

THE RIVER'S SECRET.

A lady sought the river's side at night,
A lovely lady, delicately fair;
With eyes and jewels gloriously bright,
And flowing robe, and flowing sable hair·
Fair was the lady beyond poesy,
Fairer than knight or minstrel ever dreamed;
Proud was the lady, as would lady be,
By all the land the Queen of Beauty deemed.

Unto the river's side she came alone,
That fair proud lady in the hush of night;
And kneeling 'neath the stars, began to moan,
Clasping her forehead with her fingers white;
"Oh, Harold, Harold! comest thou no more,
Even to mourn, where we so oft have met?
Ah, woe is me, the haughty Isadore,
When Harold proves the readiest to forget!"

Thus grieved the lady for her cruelty,
And called upon her Harold's name with tears;
But midnight came and parted silently,
And yet no Harold soothed the lady's fears.

And still she mourned, and still the sullen river
Rolled onward, without heeding her complain—
The cold, dark, ruthless, unrelenting river,
Whose bosom held the mystery of her pain.

A night agone, a secret had been given
Into its keeping, and it kept it well;
No witness was there save the stars and heaven,
And what the angels see they do not tell.
Down, down beneath the flood, upon a pillow
Of moss-grown rock the form of Harold lay;
Sleeping as sweetly as 'twere not the billow
That sung to him, instead of lady gay!

After a time the cold dark river parted,
And *two* forms lay beneath the sullen wave;
A lovely lady, pale and broken-hearted,
Had found unconsciously her lover's grave.
And side by side, beneath the darksome river,
That kept their secret well for evermore,
Sleep hearts once brave, that broke in life's wild fever,
The noble Harold, and fair Isadore.

Strange are the legends that the minstrels tell
Of "fairie ladie," and of knight betrayed;
But the dark river keeps their secret well,
And none e'er found where their deep graves were made;
The river, dark and sullen as of yore,
Told only me the fate of Isadore.

RESOLUTION.

Room, room for the freed spirit! Let it fling
  Its pinions worn with bondage once more wide,
And if in earth or air there is a thing
  To stay its soaring, let the heavens chide!
Away, the silken bondage of young dreams;
  No more in gentle dalliance I'll lay
My hand upon my lute, like one who seems
  In half unconscious idleness to play.

But all there is in me of living soul,
  Of high, proud daring, or of untried trust,
Shall not be subject longer to control;
  For my desire is upward, and I must
Spurn back the fetters of the slothful past
  As a loosed captive tramples on his chain;
From now, henceforth, my destiny is cast,
  And what I *will*, I surely shall attain.

Onward and upward! strengthening in their flight,
  My thoughts must "all be eagle thoughts," nor bend
Their pinions downward, until on the height
  That nurses Helicon's pure fount I stand.
Onward, my soul! nor either shrink nor turn,
  Be cold to pleasure and be calm to pain;
However much the yielding heart may yearn,
  Listen not, listen not, it is in vain!

Upward! "a feeling like the sense of wings,"
  A proud, triumphant feeling buoys me up,
And my soul drinks refreshment from the streams
  That fill forever joy's enchanted cup.
A glorious sense of power within me lies,
  A knowledge of my yet untested strength,
And my impatient spirit only sighs
  For the far goal to be attained at length.

TALE OF THE FOREST.

I KNOW of a spot in our Western woods,
Where the deep shadows lie on the rushing floods,
Where the foam and the mist are as white as snow
On the dark brown sides of the rocks below;
Where yet deeper down I can see the gleam
Of the sunshine broad on the glimmering stream,
Through arches of green, twined of leaves that shiver
To the breath of the wind and the sound of the river.

There are violets growing there all the year,
When the leaves of the forest are dry and sere,
Fed by the dew that distils all the day
From the moist green leaves or the river's spray;
And a bird with a soft, wild, silvery note,
And a sound of grief in its little throat,
Has chosen the shade for its lonely song—
To that bird and to me does the place belong.

There, when the summer was fairest, I made
At the falling of twilight, a grave—and laid
A heart that was weary forever to rest—
The heart that had broke in my beating breast;
Wrapt and shrouded in mist, and covered in gloom,
Mourned by the bird and the drooping plume
Of the evergreen trees that bend o'er the flood,
I left it to sleep in that wild solitude.

When the summer hung light on the maple boughs,
And the birds in the greenwood were singing their vows,
Came I one sunset and sat where the gleam
Glanced from the young leaves and fell on the stream;
And sitting I heard what my spirit hears yet,
And the heart that I buried can never forget;
Holy and solemn the vow that was made—
Ere summer had ripened the vow was betrayed.

Now where the autumn leaves lie on the ground,
And the dark river flows with a sullen sound,
And the white cloud of mist rises up from the gloom
Like the ghost that I laid bursting out of its tomb,
Come I each twilight and pillow my head
On the dark withered leaves—the grave of the dead,
And list to the murmur of leaves and of river,
Praying sleep may descend on my eyelids forever.

INDIAN SUMMER.

Tell me, ye whose locks are whiter
 Than the frozen winter snow,
Tell me if your hearts grew lighter,
And your hopes of heaven brighter,
 As the beat of life grew slow;
Is there, say, an Indian summer
 After life's autumnal glow?

Gentle youth, and ardent manhood,
 Spring and summer emblem well;
Ripened fields and fading greenwood,
Withered blossoms, pale and wind-strewed,
 Of life's wasting fullness tell;
And the bleak and barren winter
 Has in age its parallel.

But when all the freshness faded
 And the wintry cold was near,
When the locks that once had shaded
Youthful brows, with gray were braided,
 Were your spirits cold and drear?
Or came there a mellow brightness
 Warming life's dull atmosphere?

Tell me, for I dread the healing
  Of the heart above its dead—
Its dead dreams of hope and feeling,
And its passionate revealing
  In the bitter tear-drops shed
Long, and long, by wounded fondness—
  Wounded love that wept and bled.

Tell me that, though pale and withered,
  All the flowers of feeling lie;
That no frost above has gathered,
And no icy bound has tethered
  The strong soul's intensity;
Tell me ye can love and suffer,
  Hope and trust yet earnestly.

Let me think that calm and holy,
  Gently warm and softly light,
Neither gay nor melancholy,
Neither sad nor joyous wholly,
  But all sweetly still and bright,
Like a lovely Indian summer,
  Age may come and bring no blight.

But if storms must moan and shiver,
  Through life's late autumnal trees,
God! I pray thee, though they quiver
Life's frail cords for aye and ever,
  With the sharpest agonies,
Let my soul remain unaltered,
  My heart keep its sympathies.

Let life's fever, hot and burning,
  All consume me with its flame;
Let me die of hopeless yearning,
And a grief that knows no turning
  Feed upon my mortal frame,
Till it perish with endurance,
  But quench not my spirit's flame!

Softly bright, or wildly glaring,
  Let my soul-fires ever shine,
Full of passion high and daring,
Or the warm, soft radiance wearing
  That is given for a sign
That the soul within is lighted
  At some holy angel-shrine ;
But let not the senseless coldness
  Of a withered heart be mine.

THE TALISMAN.

What would ye give, ye triflers, say,
  Young men and maidens, what would ye
  Bestow to know the mystery
  Of what an angel said to me—
An angel said to me one day?

Ah, dark and heavy was my soul!
  Once had it been all gay and light,
  And fearing not the coming blight,
  Had perched itself on pleasure's height,
And writ its name on pleasure's scroll.

But soon, too soon, a change o'ercame
  My spirit, and my heart was broke—
  Was broke and bowed beneath the yoke
  Of grief too sacred to be spoke,
Yet eating out my soul like flame.

Then, to my side an angel stole—
  An angel with bright shining hair,
  And sweet young face divinely fair—
  Speaking with voice more soft and rare
Than music's most voluptuous roll.

"Peace, peace," the radiant being spoke;
And on my heart's tumultuous swell
The oil of holy stillness fell,
And calmed it with a sacred spell
Too sweet and reverent to be broke.

"Thy soul is dark," the angel said;
"A land of shadow round thee lies;
And shapes of fear thy soul surprise,
From which thou canst not turn thine eyes,
Lest thou shouldst be pursued with dread.

"But I will give to thee a light
Whose beams shall fright the shades away,
And make for thee a perfect day;
That light is love; and with its ray
Thy soul shall shine serenely bright.

"Love thou thy God—thy friend—the world—
And labor for thy love's true sake;
Then shall no gloom thy path o'ertake
Which thou hast not the power to break;
The wings of darkness shall be furled

"For evermore; and on thy heart
The freshness of new joys descend;
And with thy hopes a trust shall blend
That shall not fail thee to the end,
Though all life's pleasing dreams depart.

"Take thou the talisman, and go
Upon the path of life once more;
It can not fail thee;" and before
The music of his voice was o'er,
The angel melted in a glow
Of golden light along the floor.

THE TWENTY-FOUR HOURS.

ONE.

THE spell is perfect! every charm of night
Has worked its deep enchantment on the world:
Slumber, and silence, and the mystic light
Of the white, ghostly moon; the bat has furled
Its flabby wing beneath some yew-tree shade;
The owl is silent in its dark retreat;
The phantoms of the restless dead are laid,
And ouphes and fairies stay their tiny feet:
Each wandering spirit yields it to the spell,
And for one charmèd hour the world sleeps well.

TWO.

Down sinks the moon, and up the tempest rises,
And each meets each on the horizon's verge;
The hurrying darkness the late moon surprises,
And maddened winds the moaning forests scourge.
Lingers the red moon yet a little longer,
Her thin horns piercing through the sable clouds,
Then disappears—when louder grown and stronger,
The tempest shrieks, and bursting through its shrouds
Hurls down its thunderbolts, looses its lightning,
Groans through the woodlands, and howls through the waves,
Air-spirits gladd'ning, and earth-spirits fright'ning,
Wildly carousing it revels and raves.

THREE.

The spirits of the storm have spent their wrath,
The sea but murmurs, and the forests sigh;
The clouds are folded back, and the bright path
That the stars take is seen upon the sky.
So almost have they reached their nightly goal;
And not far hence their journey will be done,
And they have passed away from heaven's scroll,
Or lost themselves in the absorbing sun.

FOUR.

Fewer and fainter the stars grow, and dimmer,
Darker, and bluer the sky and the air;
Paler each moment, till hardly a glimmer
Remains of the starlight that erst was so fair.
But the edge of the sky in the east is assuming
The hue of the heron's wing dappled with white;
Yet growing each minute more golden and blooming,
Till at last—yes it is—'tis Aurora's own light!
She has come, and a thousand soft glories attend her,
To herald the sun in his raiment of splendor.

FIVE.

The last bright hue is spent upon the sky,
In painting morning's gorgeous blazonry;
And lo! with pennons of each lovely dye
Flaunting the heavens, and crimson drapery
Floating about him, like a king of old,
Comes the day-monarch—the all-glorious Sun!
His garb of light girded with zone of gold,
And all his bright and kingly vesture on.
The flowers of earth look up with timid bliss,
And deeper blush beneath his morning kiss.

SIX.

The thirsty sun is drinking up
The rain-dew from the flower-cup;
The diamond beads on leaf and stem,
The pearls of the lily's diadem,
The gem that's laid in the star-flower's breast,
The treasures hid 'neath the rose's vest,
They are melting away: oh! maiden, wake!
Ope your dreamy eyes for this beauty's sake!
Unclose your fragrant lips, whose dye
With the fairest rose of morn might vie;
Come forth, where every thing is fair,
And prove yourself the loveliest there.

SEVEN.

Yet looks the morning fair and young,
  Yet floats the rosehue through the air,
And nameless graces yet are flung
  On every thing, and everywhere:
The grace and radiance of young life,
  A "joy forever" to the soul;
A joy with new existence rife,
  And spring and fountain of the whole.
Youth! even though it only be
  The morning of the common day,
Yet holds a spell of power, which we
  May make our charm against decay.

EIGHT.

If you pass along the street,
  You shall hear the sound of singing;
Patter too of little feet,
  On the sunny pavement ringing.
'Tis the hour of morning sport,
  Ere the bells will chime for school;
At the best it is too short—
  Harder play the better rule.

Long ago the laborer's toil began;
  Long ago the townsman sought his task;
Long ago the busy artisan
  Whistled to his work, with merry mask:
Now we see what toil and what endeavor,
Haunt man's footsteps to the grave forever.

NINE.

Now the lazy urchin lags and lingers
  In the shadow of the wayside trees;
Tossing pebbles from his careless fingers,
  While his curls are tossed upon the breeze.

Comes the prudent matron close behind him,
 On her way to market, shop, or call,
Quite surprised, and full of grief to find him
 Playing truant by the garden wall.
Ah, his pace from thence is duly quickened,
 To the crowded school-room he must come,
Be he e'er so weary, or so sickened,
 Of its tedious tasks and ceaseless hum.
Soon each actor to the part decreed him,
 In the drama of the passing day,
Unresisting hastens, and the freedom
 That he sighs for, trafficks for his pay.
This, because our life was made for labor,
 And its purpose we may not gainsay.

TEN.

The street is now almost deserted,
 Save here and there a straggling form;
He looking, too, quite disconcerted,
 And most uncomfortably warm.
The shadows of the trees have shifted,
 And taken a most dwarfish length;
And one indeed must needs be gifted
 Who cheats the sun of half his strength.
Ah, ten o'clock in midst of summer,
 Was never meant for promenade;
And for the ignorant presumer
 This sage remark of mine was made.

ELEVEN.

Not much has the sun his manners amended,
 But ardent as ever smiles down on us still;
And we can be only surprised and offended,
 While he scorches or melts us with hearty good-will.
'Tis the way of some people, to make their advances,
 Whether welcome or hateful, forever the same;
So 'tis useless to take any heed of his glances—
 In good time he'll leave us, unasked, as he came.

TWELVE.

Ha, ha; and oh, ho; ding-dong, and pell-mell!
What with girls and with boys out of school, and the bell,
And the hurry of workmen from labor set free,
And the meeting, and greeting, 'tis a great jubilee!

Now lies the still, bright noon upon the fields,
  When the green leaves hang moveless in the sun;
Even the clover sweet no perfume yields,
  And every fragrance faints beneath the noon.
Yet is there something glorious in this same
  Meridian quiet, as if pausing here
The god of day looked back the way he came,
  And proudly mused upon his high career;
While gathering up his strength to take again
His tireless pilgrimage o'er heaven's plain.

Noon in the country! you can hear the shrill
  Cries of the cricket in the parching grass;
With babble of some almost famished rill,
  Inviting you to tarry ere you pass;
And noisy katy-did, that lies perdue
  Beneath some broad green leaf beside the way
Striving to tempt you to an interview,
  And make you ask what katy did that day:
The little stir of insect life alone,
Breaking the lazy silence of the noon.

ONE.

Wends the lab'rer to his toil once more;
  Hies the care-bound merchant to his desk;
Turns the student to his weary lore;
  Lags the dreading urchin to his task.
Only half of the long day is spent,
  Yet you languish for the distant close;

Foolish mortal! vain your discontent,
  Vain your weary longing for repose;
Fill the day with works your hands have wrought;
Sweet shall be the rest your toil has brought.

TWO.

Vainly are we told we may not slumber:
  The tired scholar nods above his book;
Little weary children without number
  Lie asleep in every curtained nook;
Listless belles, fatigued with last night's trifling,
  On soft silken sofas idly pine;
While their languid thoughts are busy rifling
  All invention for some new design—
Some new fancy for a glove or shoe-tie,
  Over which they muse awhile, then dream;
Fancying they hear some rival's beauty
  Lauded by the beau whom all esteem
Quite the lion of the latest *season*—
When they're rudely wakened by the treason!

Many a graver person, I am thinking,
  Should we peep, would be caught napping too;
'Tis so difficult to keep from winking,
  At this hour in summer, as you know:
Even the parson, after having dinner,
  They really do say, snores like a sinner.

THREE.

Now comes the breeze up from the sea,
  And dallies with the elm-tree boughs;
And with the waving willow tree,
Gracefully and capriciously,
  Coquettes, and sighs its hollow vows.
The locust's glancing leaves are bright
  With sheen they've stolen from the sun;
And rippling back from shade to light,
They dance now to, now from the sight,
  Like waves that stars are shining on.

A bright face eager peers between
  The lattice wreathed with flowering vines,
And with a half-impatient mien,
Has guessed the hours that intervene
  Before some joy for which she pines.
The belle consults with *Fahrenheit*,
  And lastly with her mirror true;
Then steps into the quiet street,
And gracefully her tiny feet
  Present their owner to the view.
And ere the hour has passed away,
  Full many a form of "fair and brave"—
Full many a knight, and lady gay,
In quest of pleasure or display,
  Will stalk or trip along the pave.

FOUR.

School is closed, and shouts of laughter
  Set the sleepy echoes ringing;
Girlish voices, coming after,
  Mix with sweet and childish singing.
Happy hearts! how simple blessings
  Make of joy a flowing measure!
By and by, more dear possessings
  Scarce will be to you a pleasure.
By and by, Time's envious finger
  Slyly tilts your cup of gladness!
Ah, long may the sweetness linger,
  Though ye lose youth's merry madness:
Laugh and shout—your cheerful voices
Many a weary ear rejoices!

FIVE.

Now the wealthy townsman, homeward hieing,
  Clears the look of figures from his brow;
Walking with grand dignity, and trying
  To affect an easy smile and bow—

Wishing to appear not too much laden
With the wealth for which in youth he toiled;
Speaking kindly to each pretty maiden,
Stopping to caress each his neighbor's child—
Letting fall some little drops of kindness,
On their youthful hearts in very blindness.

Pleasant evening hour! when households gather
All their treasures round the ample board;
Roguish pet, and proud and sober father,
Handsome brother, by the belles adored;
Gentle sister, like a lily-flower,
Like a tall white lily growing there,
Queen of all the rest in her sweet power—
Reigning by her beauty, unaware:
Happy hour! and happy hearts, that meeting,
Hear and give love's ever-gentle greeting!

SIX.

Faint grow the shadows that flicker and waver,
Of the leaves of the vine o'er the green lattice flung;
Cooler the sea-breeze, and sweeter the flavor
Of gardens, whose odors are newly up-sprung.
Gorgeous clouds in the occident floating—
Rose-hue and purple, and crimson and gold—
Radiant "arrows of sunset" upshooting,
Shine round the banners of sunset unrolled.
Fair was the sun in his soft morning splendor;
Fair in his brilliant and noon-day array;
But all of their glory conspired, could not render
His presence so dazzlingly, gorgeously gay!
Earth thou art lovely! and fair thy adorning,
Loveliest far of the brides of the sun;
Bright are the gifts he bestoweth each morning—
Glad are his smiles on his own chosen one.

SEVEN.

The rosy twilight of a summer eve—
When changing shadows play along the sky,

With remnants which the sunset glories leave,
  Woven with fancies of a duskier dye.
The fair soft twilight, when the maiden steals
  To the deep shadow of some garden tree;
And to the silence her young heart reveals,
  Breathing her dreams in pleasant reverie.
The tender twilight, when the soul yields up
  Its love and sweetness like a rich perfume,
Filling with tenderness—as fills the cup
  Of the night-flowers with dew drawn from their bloom.
The twilight hour, that stores the poet's heart
  With fine conceptions of all loveliness;
That stirs him with a love from day apart,
  Full of high spiritual thought and holiness.

EIGHT.

At length the twilight fades away,
  And the warm hues are slowly blent
With deepening evening; and the play
  Of shadows in the orient
Has ceased, and stars have come instead;
  And over all the robe of night
Like a rich-jeweled manta's spread—
  So beautifully soft and bright.
Now seeks the lover his young bride,
  And with her gazes on the sky;
Yet, standing by her beating side,
  Sees more stars in her moist clear eye;
And sweeter light on her pure face
  Than in the half-orbed silver moon;
And in her twining arms more grace
  Than in the white-rose branch of June.
The bliss of young love's rosy dream
  Beneath the summer evening skies,
Ah, what could purchase? Not a gleam
  Of the much fabled Paradise—
Nor promise of an Indian isle,
Where ever-constant summers smile!

NINE.

New beauty adds itself unto the night
Sweet music sighs on every wave of air;
The heavens are growing more intensely bright,
And the clear atmosphere more purely fair.
The weary student throws his book aside—
The night is all too glorious to be spent
In gaining wisdom from the musty guide
O'er which his cramped and toilsome mind has bent.
He must go forth—all others have gone forth—
To learn a lesson from heaven's shining page;
One hour of its bright teaching must be worth
The soulless study of a tedious age.
The sound of voices, and the fitful sigh
Among the branches of the "low south wind,"
And the calm, radiant beauty of the sky,
Have a rare charm to his o'er-toiling mind;
And he will wander out, and wander on,
Forgetful of his books, himself, the world—
So has his spirit into ether flown,
When in free air her unbound wings unfurled.
When the gay groups of idlers all are gone,
He with the grand, fair night will be alone.

TEN.

The faltering farewell has been said,
The lover from his love has parted;
And listening to his distant tread,
She dreams, half happy, half sad-hearted,
Then sighing seeks her silent room,
And slowly, with her faint white fingers,
Robs her long tresses of the bloom
Of pale sweet flowers—yet musing lingers,
For he, ere yet he breathed adieu,
Had twined his fingers with a tress,
And praised its wavy length anew,
And begged it for its loveliness.

Her very self becomes more dear,
  That she is fair and dear to him;
And musing thus, a single tear
  Falls from her eye, and breaks her dream.
She starts, and putting back the curls
  From her pure forehead, smiles for shame;
From her white throat untwines the pearls,
  And gazing on them, breathes his name.
At length, in snowy robe, she kneels,
  And asks of Heaven to bless her love;
And to forgive, if what she feels
  Be not what angels feel above:
Then rising seeks her couch, to sleep
Her happy slumbers, soft and deep.

ELEVEN.

The soft air is so full of light, downflowing
  From all the lamps above, that like a stream
Escaped of heaven's radiance, the glowing
  And sweetly blended rays together gleam.
A kind of listening presence, too, seems gliding
  Over and through the earth, that piercing pries
Into each quiet nook, and seeks the hiding
  Secrets of all men out, with curious eyes.
Between the window-bars of beauty's chamber,
  It enters on the sweetly perfumed air;
Touching the fringes of her eyes with amber,
  And weaving pale gold threads with her soft hair.
Lying upon her lips, it hears and numbers
  The times she murmurs in her pensive sleep;
And learns the name but uttered in her slumbers,
  And steals the tear, if in her dream she weep.
It floats abroad, through every crevice darting;
  Among the dense black shadows stealing in;
And if the breeze, in fitful play upstarting,
  Parts but a shade-tree bough, it shoots between.
The conscious air with viewless life is panting;
  Mysterious eyes seek nameless mysteries out;

Spirits of elfin power the earth are haunting,
  Silently joining in the fairy bout:
The hour of ban and spell will soon be here;
Closed be each mortal eye and mortal ear.

TWELVE.

The solemn glory of the midnight rests
  Upon the mountain tops; the golden light,
Grown silvery, and intensely pure, invests
  The earth with beauty, strangely, grandly bright.
A touch, as out of heaven, falls upon
  The key-notes of the spirit, pressing out
A hymn of awe and sweetness! as if one,
  An angel hidden in the soul, should shout,
"Oh, beautiful! that sittest on the throne
  Of midnight in the heaven, I worship thee!"
And the pure spiritual in man mounts up,
  Yet with an humble reverence, solemnly;
Expanding and increasing in its scope.
  The lone, pure, queenly midnight, that enshrines
God, and the angels in the earthly soul;
  Midnight the glorious—how fair she shines,
Writing with jewels on night's dark blue scroll.

VISION OF THE POOR.

"I HAD a dream that was not all a dream"—
  I saw the Poor, the sad and struggling Poor,
Buffeting with the waves of Life's dark stream,
  And anon sinking to rise nevermore.
I saw all forms of suffering that come
  From the unequal fortunes of the world;
I saw the Book of Death all writ with doom,
  And saw the victims to their destinies hurled.

Theirs is a woful fate; God help the Poor!
  Their hands are fettered, and their hearts are faint;
Gaunt Famine and grim Death stand at their door,
  Yet Mercy hears not their weak lips' complaint.
It is their lot to starve, their doom to die
  Unhelped, unwatched, unwept—let them not groan!
No pitying ear is open to their cry;
  And mute, stern, prayerless, they die alone.

Want has no form of sorrow I saw not:
  From the meek wretch who uncomplaining dies,
Leaving his tombless bones to mark the spot,
  To him whom want makes mad, and who defies
Lawgivers and the law to bind *his* head
  To perish in the dust, but with a stroke
Of his offending arm obtains his bread,
  And bursts his chain, and tramples on his yoke;

From the soft child, new-born, whose little wail,
  Ere it too perished, was the only grief
The world vouchsafed to her who, faint and frail,
  Had agonized and died without relief,
To the old man on whom the numbing snows
  Of winter and of age were falling cold,
When one fierce night Death added up his woes,
  And all the old man's years and griefs were told;

From the strong, breaking heart of honest pride,
  To the mean, willing suppliant for bread,
I saw Want's victims through my slumber glide,
  And heard the rustle of Death's wings outspread,
'Till gradually, as a cloud doth change,
  A change came o'er the creatures of my dream,
And wild, fantastic shapes, grotesque and strange,
  Made the dark vapor of my vision teem.

They were all shades of those who died of want,
  By thousands risen from their nameless graves,

Each phantom with the whimsey to recount
   How he on earth was one of Fortune's slaves.
As in one grand kaleidoscope they passed,
   I saw all ranks of form and intellect,
And noble men among the meanest classed,
   Compelled by sorrow to appear abject:

The scholar with his proud, pale, thoughtful brow,
   The poet with his bright but sunken eye;
Artist and statesman—each told why and how
   Among the unhonored dead he came to lie.
Strange were the tales these phantom beings told
   Of lives worn out in struggles against fate,
Pining for that whose paltry price was gold—
   Yet Gold held destiny subordinate;

A proud, stern man, with face of manhood's prime,
   Whose hair was silvered in a single night,
Had seen his treasures in one hour of time
   Taken forever from his doating sight—
Wife, children, riches—and his heart gave way—
   That high, brave heart, that erst had been so strong,
And had endured so much! It could not stay
   This last great agony, and broke ere long;

He had been poor in youth, and pace by pace
   Had toiled his way along the steep ascent,
Till he had won of men an honored place,
   And love and wealth were with his laurels blent.
Oft had his spirit fainted—still he turned
   His eye upon the goal he strove to gain,
Till that for which his ardent soul so burned,
   And more was won, and yet it was in vain;

And one—a student with a pale, clear face,
   Through which the soul within shone like a light,
And on whose brow yet lingered many a trace
   Of passionate struggle with the spoiler's might—

Had faltered in the race, and sunk and died
  Unblest in his dim garret by a prayer;
Not even a friend to stand his bed beside,
  And wipe his brow, or straighten his dank hair;

Frail, delicate girls, upon whose cheeks of snow
  The bright red hectic of consumption burned
In strange delusive beauty, while the flow
  Of life grew fainter as each day returned;
Each weary day of ceaseless toil and care,
  And strife for bread that was to eke out time;
Oh! the black darkness of their sick despair
  Shook each pale ghost like memory of a crime!

And men whose lives were spent in night-black mines,
  Who hardly knew the earth was fair or bright,
Who hardly saw the heaven that o'er it shines,
  Or bathed their haggard faces in its light;
And those who searched the ocean's deep for gems,
  Or dragged the rivers for their bedded gold,
To garnish thrones and brighten diadems,
  Yet wanted food, and covering from the cold;

And those who lived beneath the rich man's eye
  In fated Ireland, and yet were not deemed
Worth the cold charity that let them die,
  Until with dead the common highways teemed;
And England's million slaves who, toiling, weave
  Their very bones and nerves and heart-strings in
The delicate fabrics that they, dying, leave
  As monuments alone that they have been;

And the poor wretches, basking in the sun
  Of fair Italia's despot-governed soil,
Begging a pittance mean from every one,
  Or taking lawlessly the easiest spoil;

And proud, brave Poland's broken-hearted sons,
  Whose lives were wasted on a foreign shore,
In exile, bitterness, and want, that shuns
  To be confessed, since *man* the burden bore.

And there were those whose lives of crime and shame
  Began in want and ended in despair;
Wild, fierce, half-demon creatures, whom to name
  Made the world shudder, crouching in their lair;
Hunted and hated, dreaded and reviled,
  Outlawed and outcast from the face of earth,
From friendship and from sympathy exiled,
  Dreading their death, and cursing more their birth.

From motley groups of women, many came
  Who told the story of their lives with tears;
And many covered up their brows for shame,
  Shunning the mem'ry of false virtue's sneers.
These clenched their hands as if the tale awoke
  In their imperfect minds a sense of wrong,
Forcing their words as if they feared to choke
  With the emotions they dared not prolong.

Of all I saw these made my heart most sore,
  So irretrievable and dark their doom,
So much existence gave them to deplore,
  And left for light and hope so little room.
But the whole scene was sad enough, God knows!
  Though mixed with fancies foreign and grotesque;
And deep enough and true enough its woes,
  Even relieved with something of burlesque.

All, all had suffered; every wretched heart
  Had throbbed with agony, and broke, or changed;
Had borne for virtue's sake oppression's smart,
  And struggling died, or lived to be estranged,

Sorrow and want and scorn had been the gifts
  Existence brought; a weary, galling weight,
That Death had rid them of—kind Death, who lifts
  The poor man's burden when it is too late.

Alas! man's charity is oft like Death's:
  It comes when all is past that can be borne,
And to our dying senses then bequeaths
  What might have saved our hearts, ere so much torn.
None learn but those who suffer, what it is
  To bear with hope deferred, to watch and wait,
And hang for days, weeks, months upon the abyss
  Of hopeless, ruinous, unrelenting fate.

My dream, thank Heaven! is past; but I have seen
  More than its counterpart with waking eyes;
And many a mournful truth the heart may glean,
  That feels and thinks, which often haply lies
Too deep for careless and unheeding sight;
  Yet undisguised, would harrow up a woe,
And show that drops are shed from rocks *we* smite,
  More bitter than at Marah's fount did flow

CROZAT'S DAUGHTER.

[DEDICATED TO CHARLES GAYARRE.]

Oh! she lies in queenly bower, and her couch is soft and silken,
  And her maidens stand around her grouped to wait her slightest word;
Oh! she lies like any princess upon perfumed mattress, milken-
  White, of 'broidered silks of India looms, the fairest e'er preferred.

Oh, right regally and daintily the lady's bower is furnished,
And right faithfully and watchfully the lady's self is tended;
But God help her! what cares she how her bower is kept and garnished,
Or what sees she that her maidens stand with eyes upon her bended?

Heard she not, or did she dream it, in swoon she so long lay in,
That the young Duke Louis Gascon was betrothed by his mother?
Ah, she knows not—and she dares not ask even her favorite maiden,
For her sacred secret never shall be given to another.
So she closeth her faint eyelids and shuts in the painful vision—
Shuts it in her inmost soul of souls, and hides it there alone;
Shrinking fearfully and full of shame from her own pride's derision,
And enduring all the agony she striveth to disown.

Oh! you should have seen the struggle! why, her face looked harder, whiter
Than a block of sculptured marble—and as motionless it was!
And her hands, save that they seemed to strain and clasp each other tighter,
Had the frozen and the stony look by which death's seeming awes.
So not even the raiment rustled o'er the penthouse of her sighing—
O'er the bosom that was holding such a boundless world of woe;
So she looked as though a statue—a rare statue—had been lying
In her place, to cheat the lookers on, her life made such small show.

And that only the dark lashes on her cheek were black as ever,
And the tresses, lying blackly on the pillow, just the same,
You would think the mould of beauty on the silken couch had never
Smiled a smile, or sighed a sorrow, or had borne a living name.

Thus she lay, so fair and rigid, with her maidens weeping round
her—
Thus she lay, so still and pallid, when a low, appalling cry,
Such as men have seldom uttered, broke in part the spell that
bound her,
And a father's sorrow won from her an audible, faint sigh.

"Oh, my daughter!" cried the father; "oh, my darling—my
Lorenzia!
Who hath slain thee? What hath harmed thee? Ah, that thou
shouldst die and leave me!"
Then a few slow tears came stealing down his cheeks and cooled
his phrensy;
Still he whispered 'twixt his anguish, "Grave restore her, or
receive me;"
Till his sorrow seemed to give her strength, and she looked up,
essaying
Such a faint, slow, sad, and flickering smile, more touching than
mere pain,
That her father's heart was broken yet once more, and without
staying,
All the fountains of his tears run o'er in hot and sudden rain.

Yet he wept not long—'twas not his mood—his was a different
mould;
And this the only spell by which his soul could e'er be shaken;
For to all besides his daughter was his bearing proud and cold,
And men knew no other theme his softness could awaken.
So all calmly soon he turned him to the maidens round him waiting,
And inquired of them still calmly how their mistress had come
ill;
And they then—the favorite foremost—quick began the tale by
stating,
Between sobs and lamentations she had not the power to still,

That as she was gayly chatting, at her mistress' feet reclining,
Stringing pearls to braid that evening in the tresses of her hair,
She bethought her of a rumor of the duke, which she divining
Would engage her mistress' hearing—being always well aware

How they fondly loved each other as a sister and a brother—
And the rumor was, that Louis was betrothed the day before
To a very lovely lady, chosen for him by his mother:
Here, she said, "down dropped her mistress, and lay prone upon the floor."

Then she went on to say further, how they raised her up, and laid her
On her couch, and summoned leeches, and how long she lay in swoon;
And how, when they found her living, the physician's potion made her
To lie in a deathlike stupor since before the stroke of noon.
But enough had now been told him, and he turned and bent once lowly
O'er the pillow of his darling, till his lips had touched her brow;
Then went straightway out in silence, looking grave and treading slowly:
On that moment he had taken before God a solemn vow!

On that same night, by the river, a young noble walked in sorrow,
Cursing bitterly the destiny for which he had been born;
Cursing, too, the young Duke Gascon, who, before the world, to-morrow
Would espouse, in first betrothal, the sweet Countess Delaimorn.
His beloved—his *own* heart's idol—she whose soul, so true and tender,
Long ago to him was given—they would sell her hand for gold!
Oh! he cursed the wretched barter! and swore wildly to defend her
With his good sword at the altar—but he would not see her sold!

Thus he raved, upbraiding Heaven—and his ancestors upbraiding,
That the scion of their princely house was heir of wealth so mean;
That he—a duke, too—must endure a grievance so degrading
As that an equal should intrude he and his love between.

Thus he fretted his soul vainly, on the rocks of hard misfortune—
Thus he lashed his foaming spirit, till it seethed like any sea;
Till one treading soft behind him, gently spoke, "Let me importune
You, sir duke, to speak more calmly, and with some less energy."

"Ha! a listener! who are you, sir, that have dared to track me hither,
Or presumed to give me counsel as to what way I should speak?"
"You have misconstrued my manner, sir," the stranger said, "and neither
Can I tell you my name or title; but your audience I seek,
On a matter of some moment to us both—to you more truly—
And I pray you do not check me by a word till I have done;
For my time is very precious, and I have arrived but newly,
And must be upon my homeward way before to-morrow sun.

"Here's a debt I owed your father—sums extorted in the trouble
Of the civil wars that ruined many a house of noble blood;
Here, I make you restitution; it were well if it were double.
As it is, there are some millions; may they do you service good!"
Then the gold he paid down quickly, while his auditor stood gazing,
Like one spellbound, on this magic wealth, and on this strange magician—
Gazing eagerly, yet deeming that the princely jewels blazing
In his grasp were but a dream, and not his wishes' full fruition.

So before his thanks were uttered, or his stupor wholly banished,
In such silence as he came to him the stranger hurried thence,
And the noble's grateful blessing was not spoken ere had vanished
Every trace of how his sudden wealth had come, or even whence.
"Oh! my brain, if you have mocked me—oh! my soul, if you are dreaming—
Never let me waken, Heaven! let the happy madness last;
Let my glittering fancies fool me, for I swear this present seeming
Is a glory and a triumph to the anguish of the past!"

Some hours later on that evening, Crozat sat beside the pillow
Of his child, now deeply sleeping in her beauty, still and pale;
But his features were grown softer—*there was oil upon the billow*,
And a fiat had gone forth to still the fury of the gale.
He had saved a fragile vessel, with its fine and costly burden,
And he hoped in time to trust her freight again upon the sea;
And what matter that it cost him dear! her safety was the guerdon
He had asked, and all he cared for; and the purchase had been free.

But the stain upon his conscience not the end attained could alter;
In the price he purposed giving was his honor not included;
From the truth he would not vary—in the right he could not falter,
And the bidding of his manly soul was not to be eluded.
And still, not quite the time had come for priest or for confession,
And *until* it came, his life of lives hung by a single hair—
His daughter's life, more dear than his—oh, dear beyond expression;
For the world, with all its treasures, with his one could not compare.

Thus, with love and pride at warfare—with his noble soul attainted
Of a treason 'gainst the son of him who was his earliest friend—
Mused the merchant-noble, on whose mind one only scene was painted,
And that scene his daughter's death, which he was striving to forefend.
So no sleep came to his eyelids—through the long night slowly pacing
O'er and o'er the velvet carpet, watched he how his darling rested;
Watched her breath, and watched her pulses, and the shadows that kept chasing
Through her soul, disturbed by visions on her changing face attested.

But the morning brought requital; it was whispered in the palace
That Duke Gascon had been slighted by the Countess Delaimorn;
And though some refused it credence, saying 'twas a tale of malice,
One, who kept the secret, knew full well the meaning of her scorn.
Oh! he blessed the power of gold, that buys the miser's late relenting;
Oh! he praised the good king Mammon that he had such worthy slaves;
Oh! he thanked the Countess Delaimorn for her so firm dissenting—
And he prayed, "Heaven send the rival duke the triumph that he craves."

And his prayer was answered, truly! for a week had but departed
Ere the lily-handed Delaimorn took other rank and name;
And the young Duke Louis Gascon hardly seemed the less light-hearted
That he *had* been made the loser in this sort of high-bred game.
And the Crozat's drooping flower—oh, she tried to smile so brightly,
And to speak so gay, while secretly her heart was slowly breaking;
But the father's eye was faithful, and he guessed her trouble rightly—
And he swore again the solemn vow which there was no forsaking!

Crozat stood before the duchess—his confession said and ended—
All the wrong which he had done her in the well-contrived frustration
Of the marriage of Duke Louis, with his daughter's story blended,
And he waited for her answer in unwonted trepidation;

For his heart could not but quail to think the answer that *might* follow,
And his father's love could not but hope she would accept his offer—
For who that longs with all his soul believes his hopes are hollow?
Or who that thought to be refused, his daughter's hand would proffer?

Listen, Crozat! for she speaketh, and her voice is the completeness
Of all softness and smooth accent, all delightful modulation;
And your doom, though she should doom you, being spoken in such sweetness,
Would be soothed of half its sorrow by this honeyed intonation.
Oh, the bitterness of scorn concealed! it stingeth like an adder;
Oh! the canker of a wound that's hid beneath the balm of flowers!
Why, the very choice she took of words but made his soul the madder,
And the agony of her mild speech taxed all his manliest powers.

"I forgive you," spoke the duchess; "I forgive you, noble Crozat,
Knowing the feelings which a parent entertaineth for his child,
And commend them; and doubt not but your motives have been those that
In a court of the affections would be legal;" here she smiled.
"And as I have bred Lorenzia up, and loved her as a daughter,
So I still do think the child my own to cherish and to love;
And for beauty and for sweetness have I truly ever thought her
Incomparable, though less like earth than like saints above.

"But, friend Crozat, with our race is blent no blood except the highest;
Every branch, for age on age, has been nobly sprung and grafted,
Never losing aught of royalty, but ever keeping nighest
To the throne, and to the scepter, which indeed our uncles wafted.

In the histories of nations will you find our names recorded,
Going back in kingly pedigree, a proud, distinguished race;
To whose faithful aristocracy this honor was awarded,
To be first in glory, first in fame, and first in wealth and place.

"Not that I would say our blood in aught is different from your own,
Or that a peasant's son may not be nobler that a king's; 334
For virtue makes the serf a king, and vice degrades a throne;
Yet there is a certain pride of power a use of power brings;
Nor that we are happy—for such cares on our position wait,
We have no choice where hearts are played, and only play our hands;
We are not born to happiness, but only to be great,
And on our greatness' highest point our altar of hope stands.

"If I chose to have my son forsake his birthright and his duty
(For it is his duty now to keep our princely fame unspotted),
And give his soul, like other men, to worship of mere beauty,
Your daughter surely were the one of all the world allotted.
But he must wed with one whose name will live like ours in story,
Who can confer, as he confers, a world-wide reputation;
Whose family mark history's page with deeds of fadeless glory,
And who control, as we have done, the interests of a nation.

"Yet, if"—and here she smiled again, as if her fancy needed
Excuse for being so wild a one—"yet if, like the Medici,
You had so risen, by giant strides, that princes had conceded
Your right to rule among their powers, truly I might say this, I
No longer, seeing your daughter's love, could hold your suit as idle;
Yet think that *now* 'twere far more wise to check this bud of feeling,
And by all gentle arts and means its froward strength to bridle—
Believing that these now fresh wounds will soon be safely healing."

Then rising up with stately grace, she friendlily extended
  Her jeweled hand, which Crozat kissed, and silently departed.
But oh! the war of thoughts that in his wounded soul contended,
  And oh, the wild, wild hopes that then into existence started!
Did she not say, if he had won a kingly place and power?
  And could he not, and would he not? Ah, in that western world,
So boundless and so glorious, should be his daughter's dower:
  And kingdoms, crowns, and scepters through his princely visions whirled.

A name on the historic page! oh, would not nations tell it,
  That he, a peasant, had arisen to rule with highborn kings?
And will not France take up the theme, and be most proud to swell it,
  When he, her regent, to her arms such fair possessions brings?
"It shall be done!" he swore the oath deep in his inmost heart:
  "A prince I'll be, o'er such a wide and beautiful domain,
That France shall be but as a speck, a small deciduous part,
  Which I, a monarch, can shake off, whene'er I choose to reign."

And then the tears—the slow, great tears which manhood seldom sheds,
  Swelled upward from his bursting heart into his burning eyes,
Till all his soul gave way; and as a fire enkindled spreads,
  Darted the arrows through his frame of nameless agonies.
This for his daughter—how should he teach her to bear this scorning—
  How hide her from its blighting breath, or save her from despair?
How keep that flower, as frail and fair as the wild-rose of morning,
  From withering ere his noon of hope, in pity's stifling air?

Oh, how hope deferred destroyeth the eye's brightness! how it stealeth
  From the lip its hue of coral, from the cheek its sea-shell pink;
Oh, how hardly with the youthful heart the hand of sorrow dealeth,
  And how surely, like a stranded ship, the broken heart will sink!

On a couch, nor soft, nor silken, lies the merchant-noble's daughter;
Hard and cold the bed they give her, hard and cold, and snowy white;
And she chides not, and she weeps not, that to this her maids have brought her,
But she lieth still and patient through the long and wóful night.

There are many waxen tapers burning in the lady's chamber,
And the censers smoke with incense that she ever loved the best;
And a trembling hand upon her breast hath laid a cross of amber,
To denote our sin and sorrow; still she showeth no unrest!
She was ever sweet and patient, and this seemeth but the meekness
Of her crushed and broken spirit, bearing death without complaint;
For she looks but as she ever looked in pain-embittered weakness—
The same sweet ghost of wasted youth—the same half-earthly saint!

Ah, to see her thus, so fair and still, calls tears of easy shedding,
And our eyes run o'er with gentle grief, that passeth soon to smiling;
But oh! there is another grief we look upon with dreading,
And which, once seen, from memory there is no more exiling:
A noble man—a proud, high man, whose years are yet unfaded,
Who standeth like a giant tree to guard a tender flower—
To see *him* fade, as perisheth the fragile plant he shaded,
And grow a gray and bent old man, down-stricken in an hour!

Oh, long had Crozat toiled and striven, with fate his toil opposing;
Long had he pampered his wild hopes boldly against despairing,
But day by day, and month by month, his failures were disclosing,
And time, which wore so fast with him, his last of hopes was wearing.

"O God!" he said, "forget my vow, my vow of sinful wrath,
When mad with pain and stinging pride I swore to be a king;
Oh! save my child—my angel child—the starlight of my path,
And take for sacrifice all else to which my passions cling.

"O Heaven!" he cried, "take not again my heart's most sacred treasure;
Thou hast my youth's dear idol now among thy angel throng;
Forgive me, Heaven, if in her child I've had too proud a pleasure,
And leave me yet a little while this love than death more strong."
But ah! the reed was broken, and the soul that leaned upon it
Fell and rose not, but lay stricken by an infinite despair;
And the tomb of Crozat's daughter bears the simple story on it
Of two hearts—both by love broken—child's and parent's, mouldering there!

KEATS.

The tall arched windows were flung open wide
To the cool night breeze. Not a shadow hung
Between the world without and he within—
It would have stifled him, his soul so gasped
And struggled for more breath—for room to be!
And with uneven steps treading in haste
Across the floor with moonlight carpeted,
He flung his arms out wildly, as if he
Would part the air pressing too hard around,
As if even space were palpable to him,
And weighed upon his spirit with a might
That crushed his soul like iron. All the while
The big drops of his anguish stood out thick
Upon his pale, broad forehead; and his lips

Were withered with convulsions; and his mouth
Was circled by a rim of ghastly white,
Like that about his eyes, betokening
How well-nigh had the struggle worn him out.
He walked and muttered to himself, and made
All passionate gestures forced by agony,
Till his first strength was spent, then flung him down,
And wept as woman weeps—a flood of tears.
Heaven sent us tears! How would the weak survive
When their great sorrows crush them, if their grief
Were softened by no weeping? Oh, thank God,
Who gives us tears for sorrow's medicine.

And by and by he rose upright, and stood
Once more in the full moonlight, pale and still,
A statue of sweet sorrow: his short curls
Dank and disheveled on his youthful brow;
And his eyes bright with moisture, and the light
Of an unquenchable spirit. Proudly thus,
With a half-conquered anguish at his heart,
He gave his sorrow vocal utterance:

What am I? a poet only,
  A poor poet little gifted;
Yet this creature, low and lonely,
  Once his passionate eyes hath lifted
In a love too fond and daring:
  And for this great sin, O Heaven,
Be his punishment unsparing—
  Be his foul heart stung and riven!

And this poet is ambitious—
  Singing his own songs at pleasure—
Therefore for this wrong malicious,
  The world hates him without measure.
O just world! O tender woman!
  Would my heart like yours were iron!

But because God made it human,
  All these woes its way environ.

Slighted love! and slighted labor!
  Man who in dull hatred passeth
Unjust judgment on his neighbor,
  Sorrow for himself amasseth,
And in turn is scorned and hunted;
  But who breaks by many bruises
The proud heart to kindness wonted,
  Knows his jest the world amuses.

Let me live to brook their smiling—
  God! oh, let me live and strengthen;
I can bear their cold reviling,
  Bear all, if my day thou lengthen.
All, I said—and yet my spirit
  Fainteth at one burning vision—
One wild dream still haunting near it,
  Sweet with love, mad with derision.

O she looked an angel shining
  On me through her golden hair:
Her sweet eyes seemed aye divining
  Some new beauty everywhere:
Smiling out so soft and kindly
  On whate'er she looked upon;
Yet my soul but saw her blindly,
  As if she had been the sun.

O the poet pines for beauty,
  Yet he should not dare approach it!
Far-off worship is *his* duty:
  E'en the idol would reproach it,
Were his wild devotion nearer;
  Oftener for the brainless rover
Is reserved that other, dearer
  Right to be the loved and lover.

Seeing her thus, why should I love her?
O it is that fatal sweetness,
Round about her and above her—
'Tis her beauty's full completeness
That for evermore deceives me,
Seeming like a soul outshining;
And this falsehood never leaves me,
But my fond soul still keeps pining.

O God! I am all unworthy,
Heart and mind are spent and wasted;
And this struggle with the earthy
Souls of men, my life hath blasted.
But I'll nerve me up to bear it—
Be a man with men contending;
Hug the mortal while I wear it,
And hope for a speedy ending.

In Rome are many ruins, and men come
To weep in pious sorrow o'er an arch
Fallen in fragments—to bewail the doom
Of broken marble, and to chide the march
Of pitiless time, who yearly covers o'er
With dust and ivy some affecting show
Of the decay of greatness—to deplore
A costly edifice's overthrow.

And some, a few, do rouse up the dead past,
And talk sublimely to the ancient ghosts
Of Cicero and Cæsar, with a vast
Amount of fancy which deserves their boasts.
The past is a great study—it is well!
Man should look backward to know where he is:
Then let the pilgrim court the awful spell—
A pensive, salutary joy is his.

But, O young poet, stay upon your round,
  Your wandering feet beside a brother's tomb,
And gird your spirit up for slight and wound,
  Lest, like the sleeper's, your soul sink in gloom.
A broken heart! ah, 'tis a bitter thing
  To know the gentle in the world must die;
That man must steel his heart by force to wring
  From his unfeeling fellow equity,
  Or perish, name and fame, in calumny.

Each blessing has its bane, and thy complaining
  Is that thy gifts are not unmixed with pain;
So finely strung thy heart-chords, some are straining,
  And if they be but touched will snap in twain.
But oh, thy passionate love is not all slighted,
  If from some heart o'erburdened like thine own—
Some fond, weak heart, by pain and passion blighted—
  It wakes on chords long silent their last tone,
  And brings back tears and gladness long unknown.

AZLEA.

DRAMATIS PERSONÆ.

AZLEA, *an improvisatrice.*
MOZARINI, *father to Azlea, and a musical composer.*
HERMON, *a monk.*
ALVERNON, *an artist.*
Fisherman *and* citizens.

ACT I.

SCENE I.—*Shore of the Mediterranean.*

Enter AZLEA.

Azlea. 'TIS sunset on the ocean! Gloriously
Has the god canopied his purple bed
With crimson and with gold! and on the sea
The ruby richness of his radiance shed—
Tinging the wavelets with a deeper dye,
More regal in its hue than blushing morn,
And softer than the loveliness of noon;
Yet beautiful, as when from darkness born
Light threw o'er earth its heaven-borrowed boon,
And earth and ocean burst from mystery!
And grand as beautiful; the glowing sky,
With its high piled up masses of bright clouds,
And ocean mirror striving to outvie
In gorgeousness the many-colored crowds
Of grotesque forms sailing the upper blue;
And the o'erhanging rocks, whose sullen gloom
Rests like a frown upon the ocean's brow—
Whose towering crests along the shores loom,
Contrasting with their shade the sunset's glow:
Earth, sky, and ocean, make one splendid view!

Enter HERMON, *advancing along the shore, and listening.*

Her. Methinks the hollow sighing of the main
Hath wondrous music in it. The wild tales

Of mermaid and of sea-nymph, by this scene,
And this mysterious music, are recalled;
And I can fancy where their pearly barks
Will burst the azure waves and greet my sight
With their much storied loveliness. And now
I hear a burst of song, as witching real
As if 'twere mortal sung it, and I saw
The songstress with mine eyes. Perchance there is
A wind-harp on these shores; I'll seek it out,
For I do love these harps of nature best;
And they are tuned by spirits, whose light fingers
Do at the same time sweep song from our hearts,
Vibrating our whole being.
[*A song is heard, and* AZLEA *appears from behind a rock.*

SONG.

Maidens of the coral grove!
Hear what I implore of you:
If ye know of endless love,
Tell your earthly sister true;
Mortals tell her love is vain—
Answer from the sighing main!

Her. A fair enchantress! and by her frail form,
And youthful, innocent face, a very child!
Too lovely to be mortal, I should say,
Save for the hound that tracks her sylph-like feet.
Lovely! she seems as if she were the soul
Of all the mighty beauty of this scene;
Wondrously beautiful! not more sublime
Looks the great ocean than that infant face!
Such a strange loveliness the scene, the hour,
And the wild, mournful music of the waves,
Have breathed into each feature. And the light
Of her young spirit shining purely through,
Awed and o'ermastered, yet devoid of fear,
She seems as when on the bewildered sight
Of earth's first children burst this glorious sphere,

An angel spirit, spell-bound with delight!
I'll break the spell, for I would see the change
Come over those rapt features.

[*Throws a shell into the water at her feet,* AZLEA *trips toward him, but suddenly pauses.*

Azlea. Methought thou wert my father; I knew not
That others visited this lonely place.
I thought that he had come to bid me sing
With him some wild sea-melody; for we
Do often at this hour sit here awhile,
And I sing songs suiting his mood, which he
Accompanies with his great, solemn airs,
That thousands have applauded; but none feel
The music that is in them like himself.

Her. Sweet child! thy father's solemn melodies
Have been infused into thy youthful spirit!
Ere yet I saw thee—hidden from my sight
By the projecting rocks—I heard thy voice
Blending to harmony the mournful sounds
Of sighing winds and waves; and I did think
Some spirit's airy fingers swept a lyre,
Along these echoing shores. And I was right;
'Twas nature's lyre I heard—its thousand strings
Vibrating in thy heart. Wilt sing for me?

Azlea. I seldom sing for any but my father;
But did I know what music suits you best,
I might attempt a single song for you.

Her. The one which you were singing.

Azlea. (*Sings.*)

Maidens of the bright blue sea,
Dwells love in your crystal caves?
Live ye not right merrily,
'Neath the wild careering waves?

Mortals only hear their moan,
Have they not a softer tone?

Maidens of the coral grove!
  Hear what I implore of you:
If ye know of endless love,
  Tell your earthly sister true;
Mortals tell her love is vain—
Answer from the sighing main!

Her. So young, and misanthropic! say, my child,
Who taught you how to doubt earth's love and trust?

Azlea. I scarce can tell, unless it were the one
Who only loves me, and alone I love—
My father! Yet he never bade me doubt,
Or turn from love; but when I look on him,
Shrinking away from the world's noisy praise,
And breathing mournful music to himself,
It seems as if he thought 'twere mockery—
And having learned to understand each tone,
His plaintive melodies are more eloquent
To me, of thought and feeling, than are words.
If this can be called teaching, 'twas this taught
Even my earliest childhood to hoard up
Its fullness of affection from the world,
And turned my heart to nature's changeless love.

Her. Dost thou love nature wholly; her wild scenes
Of grand and awful beauty dost thou love,
Even as the starlight or the sunset hour?

Azlea. Yes, almost more, but with a stranger feeling.
  I love the lightning's vivid flash—
  The deep-toned thunder's angry crash;
  I love the ocean's stormy roar,
  That beats its surge against the shore;

The eagle's scream, the storm-bird's cry,
The winds that whistle loud and high;
The elements' most angry moan
Is to *my* heart a music tone!
And yet I love earth's gentler hours,
Her sunny smile, and song, and flowers;
I love the gushing waterfall,
The tiny streamlet's gentler call—
Sol's morning rise, and sunset glow,
Shining upon the mountain's snow
In many a radiant rosy wreath,
Shaming the shadow-land beneath!
I love the tall old monarch oak,
The pensive willow by the brook;
I love the brilliant flowers, but less
Than the sweet violet's bashfulness.
Oft when the summer sun goes down
From his high zenith-sceptered throne,
And with his skillful pencil shrouds
The azure o'er with glorious clouds,
To vail his eye's bright parting ray,
And promise us another day,
As bright and beautiful, to come,
Yet in eternity, morrow's home;
Oft at such hours my heart doth fill
With feelings strange, unutterable!
And such emotions crowd my soul
As my weak strength can not control;
And such a strong oppressiveness
Sometimes upon my heart doth press,
I long to take from out my breast
The heart that feels such wild unrest:
So much by different time and scene,
My spirit tempest-tost hath been.

Her. Sweet, young enthusiast! how high, and pure,
And grand thy natural poetry of soul!
But thou art yet a child, and thou wilt learn

Another and a different kind of love,
Whose power will be a wild idolatry—
A worship stronger than the wildest strength
The majesty of nature can inspire.
It would be well couldst thou forever keep
Thy pure and innocent guilelessness of thought;
But the world hath it otherwise; and none
May pass its confines without having felt
Its cold and chilling bitterness. But go;
Thy father will await thee, wondering
At thy long tarrying away from him.
And see! where late the sunset hues were bright,
A sullen, heavy, inky-colored mass
Is darkening the horizon. We shall see
The tempest in its might, and hear the sound
Of awful music, such as sea, and sky,
And winds, and creaking earth commingled,
Making one terrible chorus, can produce!
Haste then; but ere thou goest, let me pray
Heaven's blessings on thee and thy innocence.
God bless thee, and farewell!

Azlea. I thank thee, holy father. Azlea
Will keep thy blessing in remembrance. [*Exit* AZLEA.

Her. (*Soliloquizing.*)
Earth hath some Eden-spirits yet—though few.
O how may man, in his dark sinfulness,
Stand silenced and rebuked before a child!
Who, knowing not of *reason,* hath yet learned
To call life's mockeries by their real name;
And being herself all love, yet how to keep
Her spirit all unsullied from earth's lusts;
While *he,* with his great, godlike attributes,
Still keeps within his bosom ceaseless streams
Of every evil passion, till his heart
Hath not one fountain in it of sweet waters!

And being thus, still sneers upon his fellow,
And taunts him with *his own* infirmities;
Till life becomes a scene of wild turmoil,
Of vain, tumultuous striving to become
Masters of others' passions—while our own
Are burning out our hearts.

O what a scene!
The tempest hath begun its terrible play,
And sky, and earth, and ocean are at strife,
With winds, and surge, and thunders, discoursing
With angry voices their hoarse-throated rage!
How the forked lightnings rend the sable sky!
Revealing for an instant the wild sight
Of mountain billows and dark, shapeless rocks;
Showing me where I stand—how near to death—
A rude and pitiless death; yet I stir not,
Nor feel a thrill of fear. I almost wish
Some wave, more daring than the rest, *would* reach
My perilous footing, bearing me from hence,
To die among its fellows. I would sooner
Die in a scene like this, of nature's strife,
Than living wearily a joyless life,
At last to perish in the savage war
Of jarring human passions. I can hear
The screaming of the sea-gull; well he loves
A time like this; that his sharp voice may be
Distinguished even above the howling blasts
And heavy surgings of the heaving sea.
I, like him, have loved such tempest hours—
But with a different passion: I can feel
The wild sublimity—can steep my soul
In the stern grandeur of this lonely place,
With darkness, waves, and thunder, to impress
Its power upon my spirit; not like him,
Striving to out-noise the tempest. Vain ambition!
Yet many, O how many, strive for this,
To be the loudest in the stormy crowd

Of noisy human struggles; to be heard
Above man's babbling thunders, and to say
Their voice hath been most powerful. [*Exit* HERMON.

SCENE II.—*An apartment in* MAZARINI'S *house.* ALVERNON *lying on a couch*—AZLEA *bending over him.*

Enter MAZARINI *and a* Fisherman.

Fish. The vessel was wrecked off our coast; I found him lying on the rocks, sadly bruised. I think he will recover; so leaving him in your care, I must away. [*Exit* Fisherman.

Azlea. The stranger—oh, he lives! I feel his pulse
Flutter as quick, and soft, and varyingly
As a fine harp-string in the impatient wind.

Maz. Life struggles for the mastery with death;
The cordials you have given him will restore
The inanimate pulse, and bring the breath
Back to his death-white lips. And yet perchance
Our kindness is a cruelty to him,
If he should wake to find his hopes all wrecked—
A wife or sister buried in the sea,
Or his wealth wasted. Human hopes are frail,
And one night may have blasted his for aye.

Azlea. We will be kind to him, as to a brother,
And heal his wounds, and soothe his broken spirit,
That he may not die grieving for his loss.

Maz. He will not, child; not many mourn so well.

Azlea. I'll bring him fruit and flowers to drive away
The loneliness of solitude; and sing
The softest airs I know; and tell him tales
Of magic and of love. Would it be wrong
To entertain him thus? It seems to me
It would be over-bold; and yet last night

I talked as fearlessly as I do now;
But 'twas with one who seemed to shun the world,
As we do, father; and so I but thought
And spoke with him as if it had been you.
He was a friar, and he blessed your child.
But this young stranger must be of the world,
And I shall learn to fear him.

Maz. My child—my Azlea! would no wayward fate
Had thrown him in your path. Nay, look not thus—
I have a pitying heart, and would rejoice
To do a gentle service for a friend,
Or even for an enemy; but now
I fear what I can not explain; nor can
Your guileless nature understand my thoughts.
Oh, must *this* be? Azlea, let not
Thy heart be stolen from thy father now,
In his hoar, desolate age; but no!
'Tis blest, and fresh, and happy with thy love;
But let it not be withered suddenly,
By finding its last solace taken away—
My child's sweet love divided!

Azlea. (*Throwing herself into his arms.*) My father!
My dear father! hath thy child e'er known
A thought save thoughts of thee—and dost thou now
Wrong her, by dreaming that she can forget
Her soul's one holy passion, save the love
She gives to nature, and which has become
An element of her being! No—oh, no!

Maz. Blest Spirit, do thy will! It can not be
Evil could reach thee; follow what way
Thy purity shall teach thee; and forget
An old man's selfish jealousies. Sweet one,
Thy patient needs thy care; I must go forth
To catch some wild sea-melody, the breeze
May whisper to my ear. [*Exit* MAZARINI.

Azlea. (*Bending over Alvernon.*)
There's breath upon his lips, and on his cheek
A faint and trembling color. His dark hair
Is heavy yet, and cold with the sea-brine,
And his high, rounded forehead, has a gash
Cut by the cruel rocks. I'll chafe his brow;
He soon must waken from this deathlike sleep.

Alvernon. (*Unclosing his eyes.*)
I must have dreamed, or else I now do dream:
I thought that in the tempest all were lost,
And the cold waves closed round my shuddering form,
But all was tumult, night, and thundering,
And I know not what happened. Where am I?
This is a pleasant place, and thou art young
And very beautiful; how came I here?

Azlea. Thou hast been ill, and I must bid thee rest;
I'll talk to thee when thou art somewhat stronger.
Now close thine eyes, and I will bring thee wine,
Which thou must first partake, then sleep again;
I'll sing some low, soft melody to lull
Your senses to repose, when I return. [*Exit* AZLEA.

Alver. Who is this creature of such wondrous beauty?
Her voice is plaintive music in itself;
And she will sing to me—how innocent!
'Tis sweet to have such minister to sooth
The body's stinging pains; but where am I,
And who is she; alike mysterious?

Re-enter AZLEA *with wine and fruits.*

Azlea. I have brought that which will revive your strength.

Alver. I could now sleep; I feel a languor stealing
Over my senses like a pleasant balm.
If now thou'lt sing for me I shall be grateful,
And see thee in my dreams.

Azlea. (*Sings.*)

Rest thee now, weary one, soft is thy pillow;
Rest thee, and dream of thy dear distant home;
Dream of the hearts that far over the billow
Still love you, and bless you wherever you roam.

Dream of thy mother, whose prayers ever arise
At morning, at noon, and at evening for thee;
Rest thee, and dream of her—richer the prize
Of a mother's warm blessing than wealth of the sea.

Dream of the sister whose tender caresses
Clung to thy form in her weeping farewell;
Dream of your meeting, your joyful embraces,
And the stories of love each shall hasten to tell.

Dream of thy home, of its dear youthful pleasures,
Of the sports of the field, of the river and wood—
Thy heart shall remember all these with its pleasures,
And mem'ries rush over thy soul in a flood.

Rest thee then, weary one, soft is thy pillow;
Rest thee and dream of the land of thy love;
Absence, nor distance, nor rude rolling billow,
To soul meeting soul shall a barrier prove.

Enter HERMON.

Her. Heaven's blessings on thee, Azlea, sweet child!
Thou hast a suff'rer under thy kind care,
Who I perceive is sleeping. I was sent
By a poor fisherman of the coast, to him,
That should he wish confession of his sins
He might have holy comfort and advice.

Azlea. The stranger, holy father, is now lying
In quiet, natural sleep, that will restore
His former health to him; except some cuts

Which will require good 'tendance; and for this
My father and myself have pledged ourselves,
In kindness to the suffering.

Her. Methought I heard sweet music, when I first
Entered your vine-wreathed cottage; did I so?

Azlea. You may have heard a simple melody
With which I sung the invalid to rest.

Her. You did then sing the stranger to his rest,
And your fair hands have bathed his aching brow,
And your sweet voice has whispered tenderness,
And you have ministered to his every want
With most unsparing kindness. Azlea,
This stranger here is young; is of the world;
'Tis true he *may* be good and virtuous,
But there are few who are; nay, blush not, child,
With such a pained look; I did not mean
What thou hast done is wrong, in being kind—
But in the world of which this stranger is,
Such innocence as thine meets sneering taunts—
Being deemed by its misjudging sinfulness,
Other than what it is. Art weeping, sweet?
Nay, weep not, I was wrong; and now I think,
While gazing on thee and thy mournful face,
Not any but the vilest could withstand
The power of thy guileless purity.
I would not take thy unsuspecting truth,
And give thee all earth's wisdom, and its wealth,
For thou wouldst be the loser.

Azlea. Father, if in aught I have transgressed,
Even the world's stern code of modest action,
I should be bitterly grieved; and thou art right
To warn me of my folly. Azlea
Knows little of the world, and would not learn
More than she knows already, if to learn

Brings such a painful feeling, as but now,
Poisoned the pure emotions she had felt
Toward the suffering stranger whom she had
Striven to render happy. Evermore
I will be coy and careful, never giving
To any but my parent the warm love
That does pervade my being; keeping all
Love's tender attributes and natural cares,
In one deep, ceaseless channel of affection;
Leaning alone for tenderness and counsel
Upon one natural trust—the only one
Nature has given me—a father's love.

Her. I have been very wrong to poison thus
Thy innocent trustfulness; for there is not
A more heart-troubling spirit haunting man,
Dwelling in gloom, and shadowing the soul
With a wing blacker than the wing of hate;
There is not in all man's grievous torments
A darker, gloomier, or more hideous form
Of human ill than sullen, black *suspicion!*
I would not teach thee distrust; 'tis the bane
Of all life's sweetness; I would but have said
Beware of *seeming* virtues; yet this much
Shall be retracted, since it pains thee so
To bear the imputation of a fault not meant,
And really not existing but in seeming.
If this man be not the veriest villain
That darkens earth with impotence of virtue,
He will but love thee for thy ignorance
Of the world's sinful wisdom. *I* do so;
Thou art to me far loftier than the best
Earth's royalty can boast; and thy pure soul
Hath radiance only borrowed from the skies.

Azlea. Wert thou not who thou art—a holy teacher—
I should suspect from what thyself hath said
That *thou* wert uttering in mere idleness

The empty words of flattery. I am but
The simple child of nature; have not known
Aught of man's wisdom save that gleaned from books,
Such as my father reads; but I have felt
That I was happier in my wild retreat
Than shining with the glitter of the world
I've witnessed from afar; whose noisy voice
Frightens me into silence, and whose breath
Would scorch my brain with fever; for the heart
Beareth not many such unwilling lessons
As I have grieved to glean from thy vague hints—
Too definite for my happiness. But I
Perhaps should thank thee for advice, which now
My heart is too much hurt and sorrowing
To value as it ought. I will retire,
And weep the bitter tears that flood my eyes,
And then I may be happier again. [*Exit* AZLEA.

Her. I should have known her better than to throw
Reproach upon her actions. The young heart,
Finding itself mistaken in its trust,
Grows suddenly strong; and all its softness
Is petrified to marble. I must be
Regardful in the future, and not wound
Her sensitive spirit with too stern a view
Of the world's imperfections. This is strange—
That with her native doubt of human truth,
She still is so much pained by finding out
More than she had suspected. But this youth!
Why do I fear that she shall learn of him
To feel delight in love and confidence?
By his fine forehead, and his placid mouth,
And by the lines upon his handsome face,
I should pronounce him noble in his nature—
Gentle and just; and such I think he is;
Yet do I wish Azlea may never learn
To estimate his virtues as they are.
I would have her ever as she is—

Childlike, yet lofty ; gentle, yet resolute;
Wanting in caution, and yet innocent.
But Heaven, which will protect her, will deny
Its blessing unto me, for being unjust
To this unknown and shipwrecked slumberer.
I will go forth, and lifting up my heart,
Ask God to purge my being from the curse
Of every evil passion; lest I be
Tempted to violate my sacred vow
Of holiest observance. [*Exit* HERMON.

ACT II.

SCENE I.—*Sea-shore.*

Enter ALVERNON *and* AZLEA.

Alver. This is indeed a grand and beautiful scene,
Worthy a master's pencil. Often I,
In Spain, and Switzerland, and Germany,
Have wrapt my spirit in delicious dreams,
And fancy's touch, anticipating art,
Hath placed them on the canvas; while my eye
Feasted upon them, and my soul forgot
Its mortal tenement. My spirit sees,
With one wide, comprehensive glance, a scene,
And copies with a quick and perfect skill,
Each beautiful feature of the whole grand piece,
Dreaming the while in ecstasy.

Azlea. Yours must be a soul-enchanting power,
To bring the grand, and beautiful, and vast
Within the pencil's compass; and to give
Such earnest likeness to it as to cheat
The eye into believing that it saw
The glorious or the fair original!
Do you not worship your own heavenly art?

Alver. It ever hath been first in my heart's love;
But I have learned of thee a deeper love,
A higher, holier, and more sacred flame
Than burns upon the altar of ambition.
Azlea! thou art a wondrous being—
And I know not whether I dare to love thee;
But it is virtue to acknowledge this—
That thou hast held an influence o'er my spirit,
Which it will take a lifetime to forget.
Thy care, thy gentleness, thy voice of song,
And more than all, thy childlike innocence
Of every impure sentiment or thought,
Hath won the deep devotion of a heart
That yet scarce dares to tell thee of its love;
Nor would I venture to so bold a thought,
As that I have inspired within thy breast
A single feeling tenderer than thou
Wouldst have bestowed on any hapless stranger
A pitying Heaven threw under thy sweet care.
To-morrow's sun will shine on my farewell
To my dear, temporary home and thee;
And I have naught to offer thee, in lieu
Of what would be to some, more just reward,
Save warmest gratitude, and warmest love.
And thou wilt not reject it?

Azlea. There can not be reward more canceling
To every debt of kindness, than is this
You offer—*earnest gratitude;* but *love*
Is for a higher purpose. I can not
Accept for guerdon, what the deathless spirit
Hath for its immortal dower. You mistake;
And are yet ignorant of real love.

Alver. Since you have spoken thus, I am compelled
To vindicate my sentiments by words
Stronger than I had purposed. If to say
Never shall I forget thee—never more

Hear in my spirit music like thy voice—
Never see vision with so much of heaven
In look or action; that the memory
Of our short intercourse shall live and burn
Forever on the altar of my heart;
If to say I love thee truly, wholly,
With an undying passion, can impress
A deeper sense of truth upon thy mind,
Azlea, I say it—and would be believed!

Azlea. Alvernon, I have never until now
Listened to words of passion; never felt
Aught of a love other than children feel
For parents best and fondest—so that now
Thy words sound through my spirit; but my heart
Is hoarded up from passion. Did I feel
That in my inmost soul which you describe,
I would not let it live!

Alver. Azlea, I have thought thee, and thou art,
The tender girl of nature, full of love;
And yet you tell me that you would not list
Your heart's impassioned pleadings, even when
Another heart joined in its earnest prayer
For the sweet blessing of your love. Is this
The voice of your own spirit? Hath it not
Been darkened by the shadow of mistrust?
Else how didst thou learn to be stern to love?

Azlea. Thou art right in guessing it is not
The natural promptings of my untaught heart
To harden my soul's softness; and I fear
I am not cautious to propriety;
And knowing nothing of life's varied ways,
I would avoid all evil.

Alver. Surely thou
Hast had a gloomy teacher for thy youth;

And wouldst thou live forever without love,
Fearing thou shouldst do wrong in being trustful?
Nay, Azlea, for once thou hast been wrong.

Azlea. 'Tis true I may be wrong in fostering doubt;
But I will tell you how the feeling came.
Ere yet I saw thee, there was in my heart
A native shrinking from the world's approach,
Which vague reports of glittering misery,
And hollow-heartedness, and dark deceit,
Reaching me in my solitude, increased;
But I as yet had never talked with any,
Who, knowing of the world, would tell a child
Whether to love or shun it; until one,
A father of the holy Church of Rome,
Met me, and by his converse of the world,
Taught me to fear its hollowness of heart.
'Tis strange how much I yield to his dark counsel—
Dark it does seem to me, though I obey;
But I have thought that I have been ungrateful
From that my real nature hates suspicion,
And so I listen.

Alver. And his were evil lessons, Azlea.
If the world *is* void of truth and honor,
It is because they all are taught to doubt
Each other's love and faith; and doubting thus,
Grow proud and self-dependent; and the cloak
Of love and virtue is too often worn
To hide the soul's corruption. Were there more
Of love and gentleness, there would be less
Of all the evil passions. Azlea,
Reject such evil counsel; let thy soul,
Pure as it is, and beautiful, shine forth,
Unhidden by distrust; for purity
Is mightier to banish evil thoughts,
From hearts howe'er degraded, than stern coldness.
Say not again thou wilt not list to love;

Does not thy mother, Nature, breathe of love
In every smiling feature? Is not her voice
Ever most eloquent of tenderness?
And wilt thou, her sweet child, reject her teaching,
And find in scorn a refuge from her power?

Azlea. I am yet but a child, but if to know
That Azlea, in her simple ignorance,
Hath let a stranger occupy her thoughts
More than was coy and maidenly; and hath
Even had dreams of strange, delicious sweetness,
In which she deemed she loved and was beloved—
If to know this would give thee happy thoughts,
Though blushing at her own temerity,
Azlea would still acknowledge it.

Alver. God bless thee, lovely one, for those sweet words!
When in the world, of which you have such dread,
It will be the sweet solace of my toils,
To think of thee, and dream of coming years,
In which my Azlea and myself shall share
The dearest joys of earth! and until then
Thou wilt remember me with love—wilt thou?

Azlea. Azlea can not forget thee.

Alver. Now I go
To try my fortunes in the capital;
To catch the inspiration lingering round
The works of the great masters; and to feast
My soul with beauty and with power. But
I'll carry in my memory a scene,
And a presiding spirit, far more bright
Than any art can pencil or imagine. [*Exeunt.*

ACT III.

Scene I.—*Moonlight. A garden in the rear of* Mazarini's *house.*

Enter Mazarini.

Maz. This is a glorious night! the stars are out
In hosts innumerable; but the moon,
In her resplendent brilliancy, so dims their light
They scarce can be distinguished, but all blend
Into one paly maze of fretted gold.
Beautiful! How glorious is our earth,
How full of loveliness and melody!
The breeze comes laden with the rich perfume
Of gardens, filled with the luscious fruits,
And flowers steeped in night's extracting dew;
While every swell of its low, musical breath,
Sweeps a more earnest gush of melody
From nature's thousand lyres. O that man
Should live in such a world of loveliness,
Yet bearing in his heart such hideous forms
Of darkness and wild discord. Now the past
Is in a torrent rushing o'er my soul:
The past, with its bright pages and its dark—
And darker some, and gloomier than Hades.
Viola! Viola! how my soul worshiped thee!
How wildly beautiful thou wert in feature—
How wild, and sweet, and carol-like thy voice,
Whose charm first waked the passions of a heart
That burned in its unquenched, unquenchable fires,
Till naught was left but ashes. Even now
I see thee as thou wert—so innocent!
But my vain love of flattery and applause
Forced thee upon the stage. How the world stared!
As if their greedy eyes would have devoured thee;
And how they shouted forth their mad applause,
And loaded thee with favor! My vain soul,

Exulting in thy glorious power of song,
And feeling, seeing, knowing nothing else
But thy most wondrous loveliness, forgot
The world was black and rotten to the core,
Upon whose favor I taught thee to lean.
But bitterly, most bitterly I learned
To curse its dark beguilings. Oh! that hour
In which I learned that thou wert false to me,
Was full of wilder torments than the skill
Of the arch-demon could ever have invented!
Then how I cursed thee, Viola! how I raved,
And stamped, and heaped upon thy name
The vilest epithets my mind could frame!
God knows what my mad phrensy would have done,
Hadst thou not left a pleader in the cause
Of innocence and virtue. Our sweet babe,
When in my rage I would have smothered it,
Looked up and smiled, with such a heavenly smile—
So bright, and soft, and pure—my soul was bent
From its dark purpose; and I kissed its mouth,
So like thine own in beauty, and its eyes,
So dreamy, deep, and soft, and wept such tears
As manhood knows but once. Oh, fearfully
Was my ambition punished! fearfully
Was my great wrong avenged, when once again
You crossed my threshhold but to faint and die,
Murmuring the words of bitterest repentance!
From that hour my spirit's chords were broken;
And life holds nothing to enchain me here,
But my bright child—my Azlea.

Enter AZLEA.

Azlea. Forgive thy child for her unlawful act;
But coming out to seek thee, thy strange words
Roused all my wonder and my sympathy,
And I stood silently and listened.

Maz. Thou hast indeed heard what I never meant
Should reach thy youthful ears. But being so,
I must forgive thee for thy natural wish
To know thy mother's history. And now
Sit by my side—and thou must talk to me;
'Twill soothe the feverish throbbing of my veins,
And calm the thoughts the resurrected past
Hath stirred within my breast.

Azlea. What I have heard
Is what hath held thee here in solitude,
Shunning the world, and hiding it from me:
Is it not, father?

Maz. Yes, my Azlea;
I would not have thee hear its voice of guile—
I would not have thy spirit bear the taint
Of its impurities; or have thy heart
Crushed by its withering sorrows. I would keep
Thy soul as fresh and pure—as free from care—
As the free bird of heaven; never have thee
Know aught of any sorrow; never have thee
Know aught of any passion, save thy love
For thy infirm old father. Azlea,
I know this must seem selfish, cold, and strange;
But now thou knowest how my heart was broken,
Thou wilt not marvel at it.

Azlea. My father!
I fain would tell thee what must give thee pain,
But can not bear to hear thy sorrowing.
Thy child hath been forgetful of her promise—
Hath told a stranger that her foolish heart
Cherished his image in it; that she deemed
She loved him with the love he wished of her.

Maz. Alas, alas! that this should come so early!
But my heart whispered that it must be so;
And now I find its prophecy not idle.

Azlea. O fear not Azlea can e'er be won
From her obedience; or ever bring
Her father's hoar head sorrowing to the tomb.
O no, no, no! She would not e'en forsake
For *all earth's love,* her father's dearer love,
Or leave him ever for another's smiles.

Maz. Did I not think this youth most virtuous,
Lofty, and good, I should indeed be curst;
But a few years, and this consuming frame
Shall have returned to earth, and thou wilt be
A lonely orphan, helpless on the sea
Of human toil and striving. It may be well,
And thou and I must pray that it be so.

Azlea. O do not talk of dying; ere that time
May Azlea have slept her final sleep. [*Curtain falls.*

SCENE II.—*A recess in a forest.*

Enter HERMON.

Her. I have wept, have prayed, have humbled my stern soul
In most abject entreaty before Heaven;
Have vowed, and fasted, and done penances
Enough to save a soul already cursed;
But all is weak and vain before the power
Of this o'ermastering passion. And now
I give the struggle over! If I may
But win the love of Azlea, all earth,
All hell, shall strive in vain to fright me
From my fixed purpose. Heaven refuses
Longer to oppose my wishes, and the fear
Of earthly torments can not now restrain
The passions of my nature. How my soul,
No longer bound by vows of holiness,

Longs to give utterance to its pent-up feelings!
I could yell, could rave, and tear my rebel flesh
With fiendish rage and eagerness—so burn
The fires of hell within me. Oh, Azlea!
Thy sweet young face arises in my heart
With a rebuking coldness; thy pure look
Of calm and earnest sorrow for my grief,
And thy strange, startled fearfulness, when thou
Didst learn its sinful cause, and thy dear words
Of kind and holy counsel, teaching me
What my best days knew not of holiness—
How all these memories reproach my sin!
But still they feed the ever-burning flame
Thyself didst kindle by thy purity,
And coldness can not conquer.

(*A mysterious voice answers.*)

Voice. Cease, babbler!
Thine is a passion vain as most unholy.

Her. Who mocks me with rehearsal of my grief?
Demon or mortal, whosoe'er thou art,
Say not again what I now know too well,
If thou canst aid me, do it; and if not,
Thou art the babbler!

Voice. Dost thou not know me?
Has not my still small voice whispered to thee
Through thy long, weary watching? Was not night
Full of my haunting terrors? Dwelt I not
With thee in silence and in solitude,
Checking thy wayward nature; and did not
My warning keep thee sinless until now,
When thou hast thrown me from thee? Now I go,
But in my stead shall come another spirit,
Who shall possess thy being.

2d Voice. Ha! ha! ha!
Thy monitor is easily scared away;
Thou needest one less timid.

Her. Fiend, away!
Comest thou to exult o'er vanquished conscience?
I am sufficient torment to myself
Without thy hellish aid; away! away!

2d Voice. Bid *me* not go away; I am a part
Of thy inseparable self—dark restlessness.
I too have haunted thee in midnight watches;
I too have peopled solitude with forms
Fearful and black as gloom; have worn out virtue
With my perpetual importunities.
Nay, Hermon, I am too much part of thee
To leave thee to still musings and reflection.

Her. Oh, thou tormenting spirit! let thy voice
Rest for one hour, that my vexed soul may find
Repose from thy incessant torturing.
Is't not enough that I am what I am,
Traitor to Heaven, and curst upon the earth,
Without the object for which all was lost,
But thou must scourge me thus?

2d Voice. The object—ay,
And when shall *she* reward thee? Answer me.

Her. Goad not my soul to madness with thy taunts,
If mad I am not now; it seems to me
That my brain is on fire, and my heart burns
With a devouring flame. O that Azlea
Could for one hour feel my tormenting pangs,
Then Hermon would be pitied.

2d Voice. She would not
Yield, as thou hast done; in her gentle soul
I might wear out the life, but virtue never.

Her. Again, again you taunt me. Fiend, away!
My brain is crazed with torment—I am mad! [*Rushes out.*

ACT IV.

Scene I.—*Rome. A gallery.*

Enter Alvernon, *pausing before a picture.*

Alver. Bright being! how beautiful thou art!
Not many days shall pass ere I behold
The bright original. How in my heart
Hurries the quick, impatient pulse of love!
Dear Azlea! thou hast been my charm
Against the sins and follies of the world;
And mayst thou ever be my guardian spirit.
Lovely, and loving, and beloved, thou art
Worthy a mortal's worship!

Enter Citizens.

1*st Cit.* Ha! thou hast
Completed a new picture. Beautiful!
Methinks that face is one that I have seen;
Those eyes—the same sweet mouth, dimpled and full;
The brow so strangely pure, so like clear pearl,
Rounded and smooth, with the fine azure veins
Just clouding its translucency; the turn
Of the fine head, whose clustering curls of gold
And brown inwoven shadow a neck of snow;
The lovely arm; ah! it is very strange,
But she *does* seem like one that I have seen.

2*d Cit.* Bravo! good Claudio, hast fallen in love?

1*st Cit.* No, but you will, when you have looked on this.
Triuli, hast thou never seen this creature
Of wondrous loveliness in life?

2*d Cit.* What, her?
Now, by the saints, you're right! this is *Viola,*
The wonderful singer, who some years ago

Set all Rome mad with love. I've seen her picture
In the gallery of a gentleman
Who told me her sad story.

1st Cit. What was it?

2d Cit. I have no mind to tell it; it brings tears,
And tears shame men like us; it was a tale
Of love, desertion, crime, and sorrowful death.

1st Cit. A common story. But is this a copy
Of that same picture, gentle Alvernon?

Alver. 'Tis one I took from memory.

1st Cit. Hast thou
Then seen the fair original?

Alver. Of this I have.

2d Cit. He never saw Viola, he's too young;
She was the wife of Mazarini, who
Now lives in solitude; you've heard his airs;
They are the finest on the Roman stage—
So wild, and grand, and full of melody.
I hear he has a daughter; if she sings
As did her mother, it will not be long
Ere the world finds her out. I would go
Full thirty leagues to see her smile, and hear
The witchery of her voice.

1st Cit. 'Tis you, now,
Who talks the lover, and not Claudio.

2d Cit. Hast heard of the commotion in the church?
One of the members of a stern, strict order,
Hath lately been deemed mad; and whisperings,
And vague reports of what hath been the cause,
Have much disturbed the holy brethren.

1st Cit. Why? do they think a monk should not go mad?

2d Cit. They do believe them not so liable
To mortal ailments as most other men,
Who yield them to their natures.

1st Cit. May they not
Have passions as us sinners, only hidden,
And kept down by hard penance? and may not
The very suppression of a mighty nature
Make monks mad, like all other men?

2d Cit. The world
Hath whispered such may be the cause; and this
Hath reached the church, who liketh not to bear
The imputation of such weaknesses,
And it is said the maniac will be tried.

1st Cit. Is he in Rome?

2d Cit. At present he is not,
And I believe he has long lived alone,
Shunning both church and world.

1st Cit. And this is why
They think him void of reason? he may prove
Too cunning for them yet—thinkest thou not so?

2d Cit. 'Tis true, there may be "method in his madness;"
But I have business in the public mart. [*Exeunt* Citizens.

Alvernon. (*Soliloquizing.*)
This news affects me, yet I know not why;
But ever when I think on Azlea,
Like a disturbing vision, Hermon rises,
And darkens the sweet picture with his shade.
Oh, I must hasten. As an invisible chain,
A strange desire, like a presentiment,
Hurries me to thy side, my Azlea.

SCENE II.—*Sea-shore.*

Enter AZLEA.

Azlea. O can it be that Alvernon is false—
That he hath ceased to think of the weak girl
So easily won into love's confidence?
Two summers, one of joy and one of woe,
Have flitted o'er my brow, bringing to it
A deeper shade of thought, and to my heart
Full many an earnest lesson; yet he comes not!
My father, thou wert right to mourn the fate
That threw thy child in the enticing way
To the young heart's sweet love—for *sweet it is,*
Though crowned with wildest sorrow. I have been
The sport of a strange fortune, and did not
A doating father live to mourn his child,
Death and the grave could not too speedily come.
If one I loved were at this moment here,
To close my eyes when they had looked their last,
Long, lingering glance of love; to kiss
The breath, the last shall pass these lips, away,
As it was spent sighing love's farewell,
Oh, I could shut my eyes upon the earth,
And close its beauty out without a sigh!
Love! love! love! 'tis strange the world doth fling
So much of the heart's treasures to the winds,
Treating them as the playthings of an hour.

Enter HERMON.

Her. Oh, Azlea! have I met thee again?
This is a wilder anguish, wilder joy,
Than I have known for months; to gaze again
Upon thy loveliness, again to hear
The music of thy voice—delicious torture!
O I have longed for this; have sat at night,
With darkness all around me, without sleep,

To wish I could behold thee once again.
Day after day, I've trod these shores with hope
That once you would return to your old haunts,
And I might look on you from my retreat.

Azlea. Hermon, O why pursue me?
Is not my life poisoned with thoughts of thee?
Do you not, now you view me,
The work of weariness and sorrow see?

Her. Thou thinkest of me, Azlea, but thy thoughts
Are cold and shrinking—not of tenderness.
Why mock me with the mention of *such* thoughts?
Vainly and long I've striven, until I
Can strive no longer; and my only hope
Is in thy pitying gentleness. Then
Think of me as of earth's other children;
Sinful, 'tis true, but not without a hope
That Heaven will pardon, wilt thou but only save.

Azlea. Hermon, I see thee ever,
Like a dark spirit, filling every vision;
Making my heart's blood shiver
With thy dark smile, and lip of wild derision.
Thine eyes, so stern and strange,
Burn through night's darkness, and out-glare the day;
Nor time, nor place, nor change,
Dims the wild brightness of their haunting ray.
Thou art become a fear—
A dim and shadowy terror everywhere
Filling the atmosphere,
Whose power I can not banish, even in prayer!

Her. Forbear! say not again those maddening words!
They stir within my bosom hotter fires
Than burn in the dominions of eternal death!
If thou hast seen me, Azlea, in thy dreams,
Waking and sleeping, 'twas because my soul

Was in thy keeping. It *will* follow thee ;
'Tis linked with thine existence, and will go
Whither thou goest. When thou art by the sea,
Mark how the tides obey their heavenly queen ;
Beautiful mystery ! Thus, by some influence
Which you may never learn to understand,
My spirit follows thine. If in visions
My look is stern, or even dark and fierce,
Think of the fires that make life agony,
And marvel if thou canst, that they should shine
Through my distorted features. I tell thee
Thou canst not measure with thine utmost thought
The depth of my wild passion.

Azlea. This is why I fear thee:
My different spirit shrinks away with dread,
And shuddereth to see
The fierce, wild passions by seclusion fed,
And nourished in the gloom
Of the deep cloister, and the dim recess
Of monastery and tomb,
Till this mad phrensy is called *love's excess!*

Her. No more, no more! True, in my burning brain
Are thoughts of phrensied wildness; but say not
They are the offspring of dark phantasy,
Nurtured in silence and dim solitude.
When first I saw thee on this wild sea-shore—
So frail and youthful, yet alone, amid
A scene for older hearts and stronger minds
To gaze and muse upon; and when I heard
Nature's sweet poetry in every word,
And saw, and knew, thy high and holy heart
Beating in unison with the mighty pulse
In the great heart of nature—then I knew
There was a love angels themselves might share,
Nor wrong their heavenly nature. Such was mine;
But when, day after day, and night on night,

That flame burnt like Cain's offering, in vain—
Then like him, a strange madness seized my heart—
And then I felt a brand upon my brow,
Which I did deem the curse of angry Heaven
For violated vows. And then I bowed
My soul in bitterness of tears, and mourned.
But when again I lifted up my brow,
Azlea was in my sight; and from that hour
I have not known another joy in life,
But the dark, bitter joy of unblest love—
By Heaven unsanctioned, and unreturned on earth!
But even by Heaven rejected, I am still
Only as other men; and like them I
Might love an earthly love and yet be blest,
Had I not found thee so unreachable—
So strangely passionless and coldly pure.

Azlea. Thy dreadful glances, and thy wilder words,
Freeze the warm life-tide in my very heart;
Oh, leave me, Hermon, while my senses last!

Her. Ha, ha! thy senses fail thee, do they? This
Will be delight, to bear thee in my arms,
And chafe thy pearly brow, and woo the tint
Back to thy pearly cheek, with many a kiss
Upon thy lips of coral—ah, thou fliest!

Azlea. Away! away! Oh, Virgin Mary, save me!
Protect me, Heaven—oh, save me—he is mad! [*Flies.*

Her. Azlea—once more, wilt thou be mine?
[*Pursues and seizes her.*

Azlea. O God, I can not say it!

Her. Then thou shalt never say it to another;
The sea shall fold thee in its cold embrace,
And thou shalt nestle in its deep, dark bosom.
[*Bears her fainting to the edge of the rock, and casts her into the sea.*

Down, down, down; thy look is strangely calm!
Thou goest to thy last rest, as a child
Upon its mother's bosom sinks to sleep.

Enter ALVERNON.

Alver. Ha! hideous demon, where is Azlea?

Her. By Heaven, this is Alvernon! now I know
Why Hermon sued in vain. Look! gaze full long
Upon her sea-deep cradle! She, sweet child,
Is far beyond the reach of your weak arm.

Alver. Answer me, fiend! hast thou slain Azlea?
Monster! now *thou* shalt die.

Her. Not by thy arm;
I go to meet thy Azlea, while thou
Must tarry here alone: dost envy me?
[*Plunges into the sea.*

Alver. Was there a God in heaven when this was done?
[*Curtain falls.*

SCENE III.—*A room in* MAZARINI'S *house.* AZLEA *stretched on a bier.* ALVERNON *kneeling beside it, his face hidden in the pall.* MAZARINI *chanting a low, wild dirge on his harp.*

DIRGE.

Once, my mournful harp, and never
Shall thy strings to sadness shiver;
Never more with anguish quiver
Breaking with thy moan.
Once more sound for me in sorrow,
One low, dirge-like strain; to-morrow
Hushed will be thy tone.

Earth is swiftly, dimly fleeting,
Time my funeral march is beating—
Life and death a spectral meeting
    Holding o'er the bier;
Wo is me! is there no waking?
Utter has been my forsaking,
    On this joyless sphere.

One by one life's chords have broken,
Giving to my heart the token,
Clear and fearful, though unspoken,
    Of its wasted strength;
Now the last frail tie hath parted—
To the goal from whence it started,
    Life returns at length.

Oh, how wildly hath it striven,
Till the spirit, crushed and riven,
Waited, grieving, for the heaven
    Of the loved and lost;
Dreamy visions o'er me stealing,
Close the avenues of feeling—
    Life and grief are past! [*Dies.*

POEMS

BY

METTA VICTORIA FULLER.

POEMS

BY METTA VICTORIA FULLER.

("SINGING SYBIL.")

THE POET LOVERS.

"I WILL string my harp with its sweetest strings,
 And will sit me at thy feet,
And my hand shall waken a strain for thee
 That is swellingly wild and sweet.
Look down! look down! on the waves of song
 As they rise, and fall, and die—
Do you not see my wordless thoughts
 Like barks glide murmuring by?
Like fairy boats they are sweeping on
 To a measure slow and rare,
And a beautiful troop of aery dreams
 Is the light freight which they bear.
Does not each troop as it glideth past
 To your eye familiar seem?
'Tis from thy tone, thy smile, thy glance,
 I have fashioned every dream.
Those with the wings of shining gold
 That are quivering for their flight,
Those I wove when thy earnest tones
 Told of the future bright.
Those with the starry brows, and pure,
 So calm, and placid, and fair,
Steal to my heart when you whisper low
 Your love on the still night air.

That faint and shadowy phantom-band,
  Distant, and dim, and strange,
Who link their hands in a mystic wreath
  And flit, and follow, and change—
Those came to me in thy musing moods,
  When I sat as I'm sitting now,
And marked the creeping of light and shade
  O'er the pride of thy kingly brow.
Swell on! swell on! ye rippling waves,
  And rise, and fall, and die!
Bend down thy gaze, O eloquent one!
  While the bark of our love sweeps by.
See! see—but my hand is still,
  Which over the harp-strings stole—
The beautiful dream of our love and faith
  Is life to my thrilling soul.
I dare not trust it to music's power—
  I should die if it left my breast—
Flow back, soft river of melody!
  Flow back, ye visions blest!"

She ceased—and laid aside her silver lyre,
And raised her lustrous eyes slowly and softly
To her listener's face. Then, as they met
His eloquent gaze of answering love,
They deepened, darkened, drooped, until a fringe
Of silken lashes met the tell-tale glow
Of the fresh crimson in her delicate cheek.
He bent, and laid his hand upon her head,
Amid the masses of her rich, bright hair,
And, with half hesitating tenderness,
Pressed his proud lip upon her pure, young brow—
And raised her from the cushions at his feet
And placed her by his side, with her bright cheek
Upon his bosom, and her flowing curls
Covering his heart with a soft, shining cloud.

"Thy dreams are beautiful, my sweet Adel,
  And with exquisite grace this little hand

Has lingered o'er the harp, till its rich swell
 Brought round us of thy dreams a lovely band.
I have so learned the witchery of thy lyre,
 That I can read thy every wordless thought,
As it melts softly from the silver wire,
 With the deep eloquence of music fraught.

"Adel! Adel! how shall I thank my God,
 That He hath given such a rich gift to me?
Thy very perfectness my soul hath awed—
 So blend rare gifts and loveliness in thee!
Thou art my soul's sweet, starry, radiant light!
 Thou art the life of its impassioned dream!
I've seen thee ever when I slept at night—
 A part of my past life thy love doth seem.

"Though but a few sweet months since we have met,
 It is long years since a fair vision stole,
With deep, soft eyes, which I could not forget,
 Into the inner chamber of my soul;
And with a spiritual smile on her young face,
 Began low music from a lyre to start,
And thrilled my heart with her exceeding grace,
 And thenceforth of my being was a part.

"She had a brow like thine—such rich, brown hair—
 And just such eyes—so fathomless and soft,
And such a drooping of their curtains fair,
 And such a changing color had they oft.
She had such lips—as freshly sweet were they—
 As tremulous with eloquence unexpressed!
And such a low, sweet voice, and winning way,
 And cheek whose color never was at rest.

"When I saw thee, in all thy breathing grace,
 Stand with clasped hands by the fair river-side,
And caught the look upon thy upturned face,
 I knew--I knew thou wert my spirit-bride!

Dost thou remember how I sprang to thee,
  Forgetful of thy timid, maiden fear,
And clasped thee to my heart in ecstasy,
  Even as I fold thee now, beloved one, here;

"And the low, hurried, agitated tone
  With which I strove to soothe thy pale affright—
And told thee my strange love—called thee my own—
  And kissed that brow, so holy, sweet, and white;
And how the color came again more bright,
  And deepened on thy beautiful young cheek—
And to thine eye a timid wondering light,
  That spoke more sweetly than thy lips could speak?

"O how I bless thee! how I reverence
  The pure and perfect trust of thy young mind—
The guileless, unsuspecting innocence
  Which sought not in my love deceit to find!
Look up, Adel! that I may read the eyes
  Which timidly beneath those lashes hide—
The deep, deep love which in their glances lies
  Will tell its trembling tale, my gentle bride."

If ye of doubting faith and sneering lips
Could have been there that instant—could have seen
That momentary glance, so brimming o'er
With all the unspeakable truthfulness
And love of two young, holy hearts—both pure,
Both high, both rich in the soul's eloquence—
Your scorn would have been lost in sweet surprise,
And your cold sophistry been hushed by joy
To find love was a thing so beautiful!

That fair young creature with the dewy eyes,
Laid her small hand upon his lofty brow
Caressingly, and said:

"The happiness of my full heart
When in thy presence it doth stay,
Hath always driven every thought
Of other years away;
But in thy absence I have deemed—
And when thou art here I still forget—
That I would ask thee of thy life
Before we haply met.
I know by thy high, princely brow,
And by thy proudly fervid eye,
And by thy winning eloquence,
Thy destiny was high."

"Well, listen, love, and I will tell a part—
All that I think of in my wayward life,
Before it found a home in thy pure heart,
Secure from restlessness and pain and strife:
When thou art wearied, close thy starry eyes,
And I will cease to prate of sterner themes,
And sing to thee such quaint, old melodies
As will fill thy soft sleep with radiant dreams.

"I was ambitious once! a thought of fame
Filled all my spirit with a restless pain,
And all I sighed for was a deathless name!
By day and night that sound haunted my brain,
Until my pulses caught my heart's unrest,
And on my forehead burned a feverish heat,
And a strange fire seemed kindled in my breast
Which rose and quivered with its every beat.

"But how to win the deathlessness I sought
Was what I mused on in the midnight hour—
Until there came a grand, aspiring thought
Of oratory's irresistible power.
The sudden thought was eager, wild, and high,
Yet proudly swelled my strong and restless soul,—
I felt the fire flash from my kindling eye,
While to my burning lip a quiver stole.

"And soon I stood before a listening throng—
Eager to criticise, to praise, deride—
And poured the fervor forth, restrained so long,
In one impassioned and impetuous tide.
O there is nothing upon earth more proud,
More high, more flattering to the swelling soul,
Than to chain every passion of the crowd,
And with one word their sympathies control!

"To feel that you can sway them with a breath!
And bind them with the mighty thoughts you make!
To awe them into silence deep as death,
Or from their lips responsive echoes wake!
To hear a thousand tongues one answer speak!
To make a thousand weep with one low tone!
To see the changing of each earnest cheek,
Which flushes or grows paler with your own!

"Yes! there is glorious triumph in that hour,
That would the wildest dream of fame repay—
Thus to feel conscious of your own great power,
And thus with burning eloquence to sway
The hearts of others, as the waves obey
The wind that stirs them! while beneath your eye
All passions and all feelings powerless lay,
Moved by the lifting of your hand on high!

"And I have felt this triumph! have seen all
Hang eager on the dropping of a word,
With such a silence through the lofty hall,
That scarce a breath the intense stillness stirred!
Have stood, and with a motion or a word
Hushed each heart-throbbing, fixed each careless eye!
The shout of the tumultuous band have heard
Swell upward wild and deaf'ning to the sky!

"But when I stole away from their acclaim,
And sought my silent chamber, lone and still,

And said to my proud heart—'And *this* is fame!'
  It only answered with a feverish thrill.
And so I turned away from that I sought,
  And poured my soul out on the poet's lyre,
And much of bliss and much of pain it brought.
  Shall I tell further, love?—or dost thou tire?"

"Do the angels ever weary
  Of the strains they hear above?
Tell me how the poet's myrtles
  Shone among thy ringlets, love."

"Upon a placid brow their leaves did shine,
  But my wild heart was burning fire beneath,
Because I strove Ambition's thorns to twine
  Among the gentler blossoms of my wreath;
One great thought struggled upward in my soul,
  As the sea heaves toward heav'n—that thought of fame!
And the deep music of its surging roll
  The world called song!—its echo was a name!

"The sound was hollow, and my brain soon burned
  To hear it ever ringing in my ear.
Ambition was a mocker! and I spurn'd
  What I had sought for as a prize most dear!
In this deep restlessness I ever yearned
  For something, which I knew not then was love,
And my soul's sea a saddened brow upturned,
  And murmured ever to the stars above.

"'Twas then that vision stole into my breast,
  So spiritual, so perfect, pure, and sweet;
And all in glad surprise, I thought how blest
  Would my life be if I could only meet,
Within this breathing world, a creature rare,
  Like that so exquisite, so young, so bright;
With such a gift of song—such forehead fair—
  Such proud, pure eyes, full of deep, shadowy light!

"The vision haunted me! and soon became
A part of every thought and hope in life—
And I forgot the mockery of fame—
Its followers, its bitterness, its strife—
And went forth with a wildly thrilling heart
To seek, and find, and wed my spirit-love,
Whose sweet face of my dreaming was a part,
Whose spiritual grace seemed stolen from above.

"I went abroad—and wandered far and long
In search of her—my blessed spirit-bride;
I mingled in full many a brilliant throng,
Where were assembled loveliness and pride.
Bewildering eyes looked softly into mine—
Bright lips breathed low, sweet music on the air;
Rich tresses their luxuriant wealth did twine
Around young brows most eloquently fair.

"And peerless forms with gliding steps went by;
And softer beauty stole behind the while;
And dazzling haughtiness before my eye
Melted its cunning lip into a smile.
Bewildering sweetness slept like a still dream
Upon pure foreheads stainless as the snow;
And deep, dark eyes looked out with dewy gleam
From timid lashes lifted soft and slow.

"But not the breathing charm of glowing lips,
Nor the magnificence of midnight eyes,
Nor brows which did the pearls they wore eclipse,
Nor the mute eloquence which sometimes lies
Within a smile, nor the exquisite grace
Of tiny feet upon rich carpets prest,
Could take away the beautiful young face
Whose holy sweetness lay within my breast.

"Wearied with searching for its owner there,
Amid such haunts of splendor and of pride,

I left the crowded halls, whose beings rare
  But made me sigh for my own perfect bride.
Then in each lovely clime I wandered long,
  With thoughts to meet her in some land of flowers—
Perchance, in 'Italy's bright land of song,'
  Or 'neath the starry blossoms of Spain's bowers.

"I never wandered where the skies were bright,
  Or where the roses seemed to be more fair,
Nor stood where ruined fanes rose on the sight;
  Nor thrilled to gaze upon some sunset rare,
Nor climbed to some sublime or dizzy height,
  Nor marked a river rolling in its pride,
Nor mused on the still splendor of the night,
  But that I wished thee, sweet one, at my side.

"Three years stole down into my spirit's halls,
  Bringing rich jewels on their flowing dress,
And made them there a home, whose pictured walls
  Glowed with the rarest tints of loveliness.
Soft skies, and tinted clouds, and golden air,
  And shadowy haunts, and dimpled waves of light,
And scenes of deep sublimity were there,
  Mingled with broken gleams of all things bright.

"And that one image! but its counterpart
  I sought for vainly in each sunny spot;
Yet with a deeper feeling my wild heart
  Clung to the thought that would not be forgot.
Then homeward to my own sweet land I turned—
  Blessed be the stars that light it from above!
Blessed every heart which ever toward it yearned,
  For here I met thee, O sweet spirit-love!

"And when I saw thee, heard thee, clasped thee first—
  Held thee, thyself, unto my thrilling breast,
The wild delirium of joy that burst
  Upon my soul, words never have expressed!

The deepest eloquence that language owns—
The richest power of music, ne'er can tell,
Since that sweet hour when first I heard thy tones,
How dear thou art to me, my own Adel!"

PART SECOND.

The lovers parted for a little time—
Oh, hapless parting! Yet one had but gone
To make a Paradise for his young bride—
To gather birds and flowers to his home—
To hang his palace walls with pictures rare—
To place rich gifts and music in her room—
To load the polished shelves with choicest books,
And blend refinement with the lavish wealth
Profusely scattered through that lovely home!
And when the fruit hung golden on the trees,
And the bright air of autumn wound the leaves
Whose gorgeous hues robed earth in loveliness,
And made soft, dreamy shadows on her breast,
And all the air was full of a sweet sound
Made by their rustling music, then was he
To claim the mistress of that fairy place.

Adel was slowly pacing to and fro
Upon a green bank by the river-side,
Where first they met. The faint wind waved her hair,
And sent the leaflets fluttering to her feet,
That like bright butterflies, perched on the trees
And humming to each other, swung above.
Her tiny footsteps heedless pressed them down
Into the mossy turf; and those bright curls
Wore not the glowing wreath she loved to weave
Of autumn glory, in her idle hours.
Was that young creature, with the musing step,
Dreaming of future happiness and love—
Dwelling upon the coming bridal hour—

Her heart all trembling with delicious joy
Mingled with timid fears?
Upon that brow,
So proud and pure, and once so shadowless,
A troubled darkness lay; the sweet young lip
Would quiver for a moment, and then grow
As still and mute as marble; and her cheek
Was whiter than a lily's, and her eyes,
When ever and anon she raised them up,
As if beseechingly to the blue sky,
Were dark with an expression of despair
And an unspoken anguish. Tightly twined
Were her small, slender fingers, with a clasp
That pressed the crimson blood most painfully
Through their clear nails.
In broken murmurings
From these quivering lips came forth the words,
Telling to the gay trees and the bright air,
And all the beautiful and heedless scene,
Of the wild sorrow that had come and hushed
The love and trust of her young, passionate soul.

"Oh, shining leaves, I would ye fell
To cover my dark grave!
I would I dared to pray to Heaven
To take the life it gave!
Oh, river! murmuring river!
Flowing bright, and cold, and deep,
Can your low song sing the anguish
In my aching heart to sleep?
Never! never! earth is mournful!
All things mock my weary sight!
I turn away from sunny skies—
From hope, and love, and light!
Joy's radiant wing is folded;
It will never wave again!
Bright the hour when I met thee,
Oh, impassioned Clarence Vane!

Like the fullness of that gladness
  Is the wildness of this pain!
I was artless when you sought me;
  I was but a dreaming child;
But you woke my inner spirit
  To devotion deep and wild.
On the altar in my bosom—
  Laid I down my priceless trust—
But the holy shrine is broken,
  And the gift lies in the dust!
Not as others I esteemed thee,
  But so gifted and so grand,
That upon thy placid forehead
  Did I fear to lay my hand;
And my love and reverence blended
  With a radiance purer far,
Than the light yet undescended
  From the circle of a star.
In one glorious river gliding,
  Ev'ry word and every thought,
In its bosom jewels hiding,
  To thy soul's deep fountain brought
All the wealth of my affection,
  All emotions pure and deep,—
As all waves in one direction
  To the ocean onward sweep.
I blessed you when you held my hands,
  And looked into my face;
I blessed you when you folded me
  In a mute, hushed embrace;
I blessed you when your fervid lips
  Were pressed upon my brow;
I loved you—but oh! agony!
  I *dare not* love you now!
Why did they come, those dearest ones,
  And whisper in my ear
The words of fearful meaning,

That I shuddered but to hear?
They told me of such hateful things
In all thy bygone life ;—
They said no woman pure and good
Should ever be thy wife!
And o'er my girlish innocence
Distrustful shadows flung,
And o'er love's, sunny radiance
A cloud of sorrow hung!
Oh! bitter, bitter knowledge,
At my bosom entered in!
I *can not* love thee, Clarence Vane,
Thy soul is stained with sin!
Oh! winning was your eloquence,
And earnest was your tone,
When telling of the rosy path
Your steps of life had known!
And when I listened to your words
My bosom swelled with pride,
That *I* snould be your chosen one—
Your spirit-love! your bride!
I worshiped the great oral power
That chained the silent throng;
I loved the golden lyre that thrilled
With wild and passionate song.
And when, with half-averted eyes,
You spoke of ladies fair ;—
Of sweet, bewildering loveliness,
And grace and beauty rare ;—
And how you turned away from all
With careless heart and cold ;—
In simple, girlish innocence,
I trusted all you told.
Oh! hapless fate! oh! cruel fate!
That perfect love like mine
Should have been given trustingly
At an unhallowed shrine!
False! you will mock me with that word,

Oh! wild, proud Clarence Vane!
You'll taunt me with this faithlessness,
Unknowing of this pain!
And we must meet in bitterness,
Who in full faith did part!
Why should I heed reproach or scorn
Breathed by thy lips of art?
And yet I knew that thy strong soul
Gives purest love to me—
Can I not tell a star in heaven
From a star in the sea?
I feel that did an angel sit
And smile upon my brow,
No holier your tenderness
Could be to me than now;
But still I cast that love away—
I banish my sweet trust—
I can not soil my soul's white wings
By stooping them to dust!
If your great mind has been for years
In earthly fetters bound—
If you have stooped your lofty flight,
Base fires to flutter round—
What! though from your soiled pinions
You shake the groveling weight;—
What! though you now soar to the stars,
I can not be your mate;
Ay! deck your glittering palace
With a lover's gentle pride—
And dream of wild devotion—
And murmur of your bride—
Oh! proud and passionate Clarence!
You will never call me wife!
Earth is mournful as the coffin,
And pale sorrow shrouds my life!"

The beautiful young mourner hid her face
In her small hands, and sank upon the earth.

Her tresses stole to kiss the silvery moss,
And her white dress laid daintily and light
Upon bright, crisping leaves—the river sang—
The sky was soft, and fresh, and delicate—
The breeze went by, and its invisible wings
Were laden with perfume and melody—
They were a mockery!

Her lip was mute,
But there was something fraught with agony
In the still drooping of her slender form,
And the white face lying in her cold hands.

The sun went down and the wind asleep,
And the sky shut its twilight eyelids close,
While evening made her toilette. She came forth,
Shining all over with soft, radiant gems,
And eloquent in peace and loveliness;
The dimpling bosoms of the silver waves
Swelled full of melody in praise of her,
And the dark shadows crept beneath the trees
To hide away from her clear, azure eyes.
Those deep, still eyes were on the stricken girl—
The pure, proud, beautiful girl, whose first wild grief
Was knowledge of the evil in man's heart:
An agony awoke the bright young dreams
Which lay within her bosom, thrilled with bliss,
And turned them into sorrows, when her soul
Bent, shuddering, to hear the words of friends
Blending *his* name with images of sin
She had not known existed. Him—oh! *him!*
To whom she gave such trust and reverence!
Such perfect, earnest, spiritual love!
Her heart shrank back from the black altar-place
Where its sweet wealth was laid—she could not give
Her sacred offerings where unholy fires
So long had burned! Her very artlessness
And innocence of evil caused her grief!

So bitterly came knowledge to a heart
All radiant with purity and love,
And thrilling with wild music—like a harp
Just touched in heaven and sent, quivering
With its unutterable melody, to earth.

The starry influence of the shining night,
And the low murmur of the passing waves,
Soothed, like a blessing, the wild, aching grief
Of the sweet, desolate mourner. Tenderly
The starlight stole to kiss her pallid brow,
The trees reached down their arms caressingly,
And the bright river bade her not to grief
In tones of gentleness untaught by art.
The beautiful love shattered so cruelly
By earthy fingers, here seemed proffered her
By the sweet angel-spirits of the night.
Pale, placid, and subdued, the young girl rose—
Her sweet face lifted to the sapphire sky,
And her dark, mournful eyes surpassing thought
In their deep, pleading eloquence, upraised—
And softly folding her white, slender hands
Upon her weary bosom, prayed for peace!

PART THIRD.

"Break not! break not! break not, O mighty heart,
With this fierce anguish rending all thy strings!
Back! agonizing fires which from it start,
Ere this wild torture which my spirit wrings,
Shows itself on my brow or in my eye—
Back! back! into my heart! ye may burn there
Till every feeling doth in ashes lie,
But not a trace of pain my brow shall wear!

"To find *her* false! oh, anguish unexpressed!
Be still, proud heart, be still! when will this burst

Of awful agony pass from my breast?
  This suffering racking me must be the worst
Of mental pain that man can live and bear!
  Another pang would kill me; and to die,
And let *her* know the depth of my despair—
  Better live on in endless agony!

"False! false! O God of heaven! is this so?
  And has another kissed that brow so bright,
And held those tiny hands of moulded snow,
  And drank from those soft eyes their dewy light!
Peace, tortured soul! why did I dream of her
  For years and years before I saw her face?
Why did my fiery soul its proud depths stir
  To give to her alone its hallowed place?

"Burn on, fierce fire, in my consuming heart,
  Till every thought of her—till every dream
And every hope in which she had a part
  Have perished in thy fearful, molten stream.
Ashes! ashes! ashes alone are left!
  Each feeling and each passion have expired!
The fire of this day's anguish has bereft
  My heart of every thing it once desired.

"Tears? no, my tears are at their fountain dried—
  It sends no dew to cool my burning eyes;
The only passion that remains is pride,
  And that upon my brow in mockery lies.
Now I can taunt her! I can look unmoved
  Upon the loveliness a star might wear!
Can mock her with the deathless love thus proved,
  While writhing sneers my lip and brow shall bear.

"And life, henceforth, shall be a hollow sound—
  The springs which all its arrogance control—
Its emptiness—its nothingness I've found!
  No gentle thrill shall ever move my soul!

Bright dreams and lovely visions, ye are gone!
My once high heart lies burnt upon your shrine!
Oh, mockery! that I should deem that one
Of truth and purity could e'er be mine!

"Ah! glorious aspirations, where are ye?
Oh, radiant hopes and blest, where have ye flown?
Oh, heart! most mighty heart, once proud and free?
Oh, starry dream of love? all gone! all gone!
A dumb, cold, aching hollow is your grave—
No beautiful emotion there doth dwell!
The holiest, highest love that man e'er gave
I lost when I lost thee, oh, false Adel!

"But shall I mourn thee or thy treachery?
Am I a *woman* to bewail my fate?
Shall I sigh over this great misery,
And of my sorrow piteously prate?
No! every tone shall freeze like dropping ice,
And she shall shrink from my cold, steady eye,
And dainty scorn my chosen words shall spice,
While mockery upon my lip doth lie!"

Gorgeous and glowing, from the silver lamp
Depending from the ceiling, fell the light
Over the luxury of that rich room,
Deepening the roses blooming in the tuft
Of the soft, yielding carpet—lighting up
With golden glory the emblazoned names
Glittering o'er the array of rare, choice books
On the dark, polished shelves—kissing the brows
Of lovely statues, smiling from each niche
Most gloriously like life—and lingering
Over rich paintings and bright, perfumed flowers
Drooping in antique vases—glowingly
The soft light flooded the magnificent scene.
Beneath the sparkling lamp the speaker stood;
The fatal missive of the gentle girl

Lay on the floor, trodden beneath his feet.
Sculpture a hollow form of cold, still stone,
Transparent, stern, immovable, and pale,
And kindle a wild, burning fire within—
So did the mighty pain burn in his heart,
And glow through his still features, as he stood
With folded arms and high, proud, pallid form.
His voice had died away 'mid shadows dim
In distant nooks of the luxurious room,
And silently the fire consumed within him.

Then spirits came to haunt the hollow void
Where once a great heart throbbed—pride and despair
Wrestled within his bosom, and his face
Grew fearfully contorted with their might.
Now Pride looked out from his deep, flashing eye,
And sat a moment on his haughty brow;
Anon Despair gleamed wildly in his glance,
And shrieked and quivered on his ashy lip.

Another spirit, wilder than the rest,
Then rose within him—Shadow of the Past—
And taunted him with hateful memories.
Moaning in bitterness, the proud man sank
Upon the floor in crouching agony,
And pleaded with those mocking shapes of sin
To leave him to the fearful punishment
Of his own hollow loneliness—in vain!
His brow lay on the letter he had cast
In madness 'neath his feet—his hands were pressed
Convulsively o'er his hot, tearless eyes—
There was no "angel presence" near him then!
The words his forehead touched had broke forever
The silvery chain that bound his wayward soul
To purity, and peace, and innocence!
Wildly he pleaded with rebuking shapes
That rose before the vision of his soul!
Insensible things, glittering in that gay room,

Seemed shaken by his low, wild, aching tones:
The flowers bent down, and drooped, and fainting, died:
A harp-string snapped and broke, and a lute sighed;
Dark shadows shivered in the fitful light,
And all the crystals in the shining lamp
Shut up their sparkling eyes, and looked no more
Upon his prostrate anguish—all was dark.
Still struggled through the gloom his passionate voice!

"Oh! mocking memories! why haunt me now?
Oh! phantoms of the past, that round me rise,
Ye know not how your presence burns my brow
And taunts to agony my shrinking eyes!
Leave me! oh, leave me! ye reproachful band,
Why do you stand and gaze on my despair?
Why do you circle round me, hand-in-hand,
Pale, saddened spirits, once so bright and fair?

"I know ye all! I know who wrought your fate—
This retribution is too great to bear!
If ye are pale, and sad, and desolate—
Look on! and shudder at my great despair!
Ye will not pity me! such as I gave
Of cold, false, hollow pretense, give you me!
Away! away! pale phantoms of the grave!
Taunt not the wildness of my misery.

"Oh, Ina! Ina! vision white and fair!
How pale and sweet thou dost before me rise;
I hear the pleading that thy lip doth bear—
I see the agony in those soft eyes!
And now I see thee mute and still in death,
Thy golden curls dark with the dripping wave,
Thy young, sweet lip robbed of its loving breath,
Thy fairy form in a dishonored grave!

"And thou, proud, broken-hearted Isidore!
Thy wild reproach, thy scorn, and thy strange curse—

Away! away! this suffering is more
  Than thy wild prayer invoked for me, far worse
Than any nature less than mine could brook,
  Or even dream of in its maddest power!
Away! with that dark, scornful, fearful look,
  And leave me to the anguish of this hour!

"Ye haunting spirits of the past, away!
  Eyes once so soft now burn my very soul!
I can not hope—I can not sleep—nor pray!
  Wild phantoms have me in their dark control.
Pride! pride! where have you flown, my boasted pride?
  My brain is agony—my soul is hell!
In vain my soul these visions has defied—
  Oh, this despair—Adel! Adel! Adel!"

PART FOURTH.

By a Venetian window stood Adel—
Her soft, deep eyes turned with a pensive look
Upon a sunset, rarely beautiful.
One round and snowy arm held back the folds
Of a rich, crimson curtain, whose warm glow
Tinged with a deeper color the young cheek
Resting against the casement.

Purer still,
And holier than ever, was her brow—
Her eyes were deeper and more angel-like,
And her sweet lip more placid and less bright—
Her form more fragile even than of yore—
Her manner so subdued and spiritual—
Herself the exquisite embodiment
Of purity, and loveliness, and grace—
So sadly, softly beautiful she stood.

The muffled echo of a coming step,
Wrapped up in roses from the Persian loom,

Stole through the fair apartment; but Adel
Listed not the soft echo 'mid its flowers.
Her thoughts were with her eyes, on the gay sky—
Her dreams were with the sunset—purple, and gold,
And crimson palaces she built in air,
With her wild fancies for the artisans.
And when she thought what spirit she would choose
To dwell with her beneath their gorgeous roofs,
She sighed, and her lip quivered mournfully.
But still she mused on beautiful, bright things—
With not a throb of her impassioned heart—
With not a tremble of her delicate hand—
Nor quiver of the lashes sweetly raised—
Nor startling of the color in her cheek,
To tell her that HE stood almost beside her—
That the dark eyes of Clarence Vane were fixed
Upon the eloquence of her fair face!

Stilly he stood, and read her musing mood.
He saw that all was beautiful and pure—
That her young heart had turned away from him
Because he was unworthy—that her soul
Was blessed with holy peace—the blessed peace
That was denied unto his fevered brain.
Wild waves of bitterness swept o'er his soul;
Her quiet mood was madness to his own—
Her placid face was torture, when his own
Had grown so furrowed in his agony!
One burning will, to crush her by the weight
Of scorn and pride, held his wild passions down—
Coldly and mockingly his dark eye smiled,
And his lip curled maliciously—

"Adel!"

The fair girl started from her rosy dreams,
And the faint flush upon her cheek went down
At the first sound of that cold, mocking voice.
Love! O love! how fearful is thy power!

She had thought that Clarence was no more
Than the wild wind to her—that every link
That bound her soul to his had broken been
By the abhorrence of his sinful past—
That the dark, struggling anguish of her soul
Had been subdued forever—yet oh! now,
The very instant that her eyes met his,
She FELT the spell upon her! A strange thrill
Crept round her sinking heart—the weary past
Was all forgotten, and she only felt
His presence! Why stood he thus and smiled?
The life seemed fainting in her heart; her lip
Spoke not, but with uneven step she came
And leaned her forehead on his throbless breast!
No word, and no caress! And summoning strength
She lifted up her face and looked in his.
Cold were his eyes, and stern his altered brow,
And his fine lips were curled into a sneer.
He thought to crush with coldness and contempt
The gentle spirit of the gifted girl;
And for a moment she was powerless
With sorrow, not with dread. She clung to him
With icy and faint grasp, her large, strange eyes
Fixed on his face, and murmured to herself,
Slowly and soft, as in a painful dream:

"He greets me with no loving word—
His brow is stern with pride;
The stars our passionate vows have heard,
Yet knows he not his bride!
My brow with anguish is distressed—
My heart is fainting in my breast;
Yet soothes he not, and speaks he not!
I know—I know I am forgot!"

Unconscious of her words was the young girl,
In that dark moment of bewilderment
When love came back, unbidden, to her heart;

It was as well; the evil in *his* breast
Had quenched the starry light of love forever;
The fate of one so good and beautiful
Must not be blended with so dark a fate.
With a chill, bitter smile, he answered her:

"I much regret this knowledge comes so late;
I did not dream your missive was a jest!
But even in jest there sometimes lurks a fate,
Preventing love like ours from being blest;
And as I deemed you earnest, I had thought
It was as well to seek another bride.
The message with such just rebukings fraught
Was only play—you did not mean to chide?

"Most highly I approve your faith and trust;
Nor caught nor held by slander's secret spring—
What was it about stooping to the dust—
Or 'bout an eagle with a dirty wing?
Have you repented of your cruelty?
Have you forgotten what you so detest?
And do you prize *me* more than *purity?*
I can not realize I am so blest!

"But think not, pretty puritan, I could
Require the sacrifice that you must make
Of friends' approval and of all that's good
For a low lover's most unworthy sake.
No! no! the proffered bliss I must decline,
Though it should break my heart to say farewell!
Yet, *if for love of me* you still should pine,
I'll wed thee out of *pity*, fair Adel!"

Back from his bosom had the maiden sprang
As his first words startled her 'wildered ear,
And stood up calm and strong, but deathly pale;
And when his sneering lips grew bitterer still,
Her slender form grew stronger in its pride;

And the bright, haughty crimson in her cheek
Burnt clear and beautiful; and her rich lip
Curled outward in resentment, sweet and full.
And when he ceased, she stood and gazed on him
In silent scorn, most deep and withering.
Never a star looked on a petty flame
With clearer luster than her steady eye
Answered the mock disdain that quailed in his!
Never a queen so wore her regal crown
As she her conscious purity and pride!
The tumult in his breast lay hushed and shamed
Before that peerless majesty of mien—
The lip that breathed of *pity* paled with awe
Of the bright being that before him stood,
So lofty in her beauty and her scorn!
But still pride struggled with a sense of shame,
And with a husky voice he would have spoke
Still further his unmanly bitterness;
But with a matchless wave of her white hand
And flashing eye, she uttered, clear and quick—

"No more! no more! the spell is broke
Which held me in its dizzy sway—
My dream of thee at last has woke
To see thee in revealing day!
I can not mourn the spell is past
Which held my spirit's powers fast—
I can not mourn the real light—
I scorn thee from my waking sight—
Away! away

Obedient to that gesture of command,
From her proud, glorious presence, with no word,
No sigh, and no farewell, young Clarence turned.
The souls once blent in seeming perfectness
Were riven apart forever—evermore!
Earth—earth! thy mystery—thy agony!

In the deep twilight, as it gathered 'round,
Adel stood where he left her, with her hands
Pressed tight upon her heart, and murmuring
In one same accent low, " 'Tis o'er—'tis o'er!"
And from that hour she gathered up her strength,
And grew more lofty and more beautiful,
With all her pride of genius and of soul.
She trusted not the world, nor hated it;
But with a peerless manner, and a brow
Like snow in coldness and in purity,
She walked amid its throngs, confiding not,
But loved and wondered at for starry gifts—
A marble casket, exquisitely fair,
With priceless jewels glittering therein!
At times she swept her lyre with hand divine,
And eagerly the world listed the strains
Thrilling its heart with their rare eloquence—
So sweet, and soft, and passionate, and full;
And through the fineness of each delicate note
A finer tone lingered on the 'tranced ear—
A music mournfully and softly strange,
Like a faint dirge played upon higher keys,
Or tear-drops falling on the spirit's wires.

Have you ne'er seen a palace grand and high,
And decked within by many costly things?
Pictures of beauty and bright burning lamps,
And books of wisdom, and sweet, pleasant flowers,
And many tall, fair mirrors, giving back
A thousand times the splendor that they saw?
Like such a palace was proud Clarence Vane
Before he met his beautiful Adel.
But the fair habitants who should have been
Within so bright a dwelling, had gone out,
And lowly slaves were rioting within.
Virtue and Peace, and Truth and Eloquence
Were frighted from its chambers—even Pride
And stern Ambition fled the revelry

Of the dark slaves they could not fraternize.
Passion, and Selfishness, and all their brood
Of tyrant evils feasted in that home,
And tore the books of wisdom, and defaced
The lovely pictures Fancy had designed,
And crushed the flowers of Purity, and quenched
The burning lamps of Genius where they hung!
But a sweet angel-visitant then came,
And with the aweing power of purity
Walked through the palace, and the evils fled.
With graceful hand the pictures she retouched,
Re-lighted the dark lamps, re-wrote the books,
And breathed new perfume in the withered flowers;
And wheresoe'er she walked, the mirrors gave
Only her own fair image pure and bright;
And this sweet angel was Spiritual Love!

When she departed, desolate Despair
Touched his wild torch to all the lovely scene;
And while the flames rose over all within,
Stood 'mid the fearful ruin, Samson-like,
The maddened instrument of his own death.
Yet who that stood and on that palace gazed,
With its proud, marble front so calm and cold,
Would even dream that all was dark within—
All hollow, dreary, charred, and tenantless—
Save by the ghosts of past magnificence!
But thus it was with Clarence, since the hour,
When doubly desolate, rebuked, and still,
He went forth from the presence of his love.
His mighty heart became the sepulcher
Holding the ashes of its own dead friends,
And haunted by pale shadows of the past;
While mind, like a dumb slave, sat at the door,
That none might know the desolation there!

If the young flowers of Adel's high heart
Were laid upon a shrine that withered them,

Should no more bloom be gathered? While her hand
With mournful sweetness swept her silver lyre,
Attracted by its angel melody,
A spirit came and bended at her feet,
With earnest love and gentle reverence—
A spirit worthy to commune with hers—
Gifted and eloquent, and full of truth!
And grateful for the homage offered her,
While all her soul quivered with intense joy,
She yielded up the jewels of the love
That would not blend with darkness—and received,
With blessings and with prayers and earnest trust,
A love and tenderness as deep and pure
As the rich light that broods around a star.

LELLA.

Softly sleeping, softly sleeping,
Where the graceful vines are creeping
With their tendrils intertwining—
Where the dew all day is shining—
Where a limpid stream is wending,
And one aged tree is bending,
And the gentle flowers are weeping,
Softly sleeping, softly sleeping,
Lella lies.

Pale stars glisten, pale stars glisten,
Blossoms bend their heads to listen—
In the old tree winds are toning
Rustling music, sad and moaning—
Moonbeams through the shades are beaming
Where a cold white stone is gleaming—

Tell us why where vines are creeping,
Softly sleeping, softly sleeping,
Lella lies?

Oft in childhood, oft in childhood,
Tired of rambling through the wildwood,
In these very sweet recesses
Lella used to braid her tresses.
When each curl and flower is linking,
Into slumber watch her sinking—
Tiny feet from white robe peeping,
Softly sleeping, softly sleeping,
Lella lies.

Now a maiden, now a maiden,
Still her curls with flowers are laden,
Still she sits where buds are springing,
With the wild birds gayly singing;
Love-light on her brow is beaming—
Watch her in her woman-dreaming—
Clouds and sunshine, smiles and weeping—
Softly sleeping, softly sleeping,
Lella lies.

Like a flower, like a flower
Fading in its woodland bower,
Lella's form grew light and lighter,
And her young cheek white and whiter.
Now no more where birds are singing,
Her sweet, merry laugh is ringing,
Nor where fair things watch are keeping,
Softly sleeping, softly sleeping,
Lella lies.

Waking never, waking never,
Lella sleepeth now forever.
Pale, and cold, and still she lieth—
Streamlet calls and bird replieth—

Still to-morrow and to-morrow
Drooping willows weep in sorrow—
Yet where glancing waves are leaping,
Softly sleeping, softly sleeping,
Lella lies.

ANGELS.

I DREAMED that I was floating in a tiny boat and fair—
Floating—floating—softly floating through the blue and dreamy air!
And my boat was but a shining cloud of pure and pearly white,
With its sails and graceful curvings tinted with a golden light,
And the gentle breath of heaven moved it murmuringly along,
With a ripple and a motion soft as swelling of a song.
Sweetly, sweetly rose the music from the undulating air;
Softly to its rise and falling moved the snowy boat and rare;
While, within its bosom resting did I dreaming float along,
Till my heart kept time in beating to the motion and the song.
Ah, how dizzily delicious! my wild pulse would not be still!
Floating—floating—every motion through my being sent a thrill!
Loosened were my flowing tresses, and they streamed upon the air
Till they seemed to catch the glory that was glowing everywhere;
And my form was draped in tissue, half the lily, half the rose—
Just the color that the sunset through a pearly vapor throws!
And a wreath like shining starlight was around my forehead flung,
And my lips were softly singing what the azure ripples sung.
How I wondered why I floated through the ether's dizzy height—
Why my garments and my tresses grew so beautifully bright!
And the more and more I wondered all the music had a sound
As if "*angel—angel—angel!*" was murmuring all around.
Half delighted and half trembling, full of sweet, uncertain dread,
I unconsciously repeated what the whisper round me said.
Angel? murmured I, inquiring, when I saw, with sudden start,

That which sent the glad blood leaping in a torrent to my heart:
Softly on my shoulders folded lay a pair of glittering wings,
Pure and beautiful, and glancing like to living, breathing things!
Oh! I longed yet feared to wave them, for it seemed as if they slept,
Though my shining tresses kissed them and upon their brightness crept.
Onward, onward moved my bright boat through the dreamy azure air—
Then I saw around me, rippling through the ether everywhere,
Many and many a pearly vessel with its gleam of golden light;
And in each one, softly singing, sat an angel pure and bright.
Their wings like mine were folded, and their wreaths had such a glow,
But their starry eyes moved never from the living world below.
Then I knew that they were angels—guardian angels of the earth—
That each angel watched a spirit from the moment of its birth!
That they hovered o'er them ever, in the day and in the night,
Looking ever at their spirits with their eyes of living light.
Each one had the pleasant power to bestow some gift of grace
On the soul which it was guarding in its earthly dwelling-place.
And no heart, however sinning, beat within a human breast,
But that angel-gift still lingered like a holy thing and blest!
Then methought I saw the spirit that thenceforth was in my care—
'Twas a bright and blessed infant, pure, and beautiful, and fair,
Sleeping on its mother's bosom, with its eyes of dewy blue
From their half-unclosing fringes like deep starlight shining through;
With its cheeks as soft as velvet, and its ringlets of brown hair
Lying on its blue-veined temples and its forehead baby-fair.
Oh! the darling was so beautiful! the mother's gaze of pride
Grew dim with dewy lovingness—the tears she could not hide
Stole to her drooping lashes, and she murmured a low prayer
That her babe might be forever thus—sinless, pure, and fair.
Then I laid my angel-gift on the heart of the little child,
And she opened her eyes so sweetly in her mother's face and smiled.
It was not pride or beauty, or a princess' diadem,
But the pearl of changeless modesty—a purer, holier gem.
Then an angel glided by me whose gaze so still and deep
Was in a silent chamber where a young girl lay asleep.

That chamber was familiar, and I could not turn away—
'Twas my own deserted being that upon the couch yet lay.
I watched with breathless eagerness—from 'neath her starry wing,
The angel took a warbler, a bright and radiant thing,
And with a tearful blessing she sent it down to rest
On the spirit-chords forever within the sleeper's breast.
Then darkness came upon me, the brightness left no trace,
Down, down I felt me sinking through dark and dizzy space,
Till I lay within my chamber, and the moonlight's silver gleam
Startled me from my slumber, and I knew it was a dream!
And now since that sweet vision, forever at the sight
Of any thing that's beautiful, or eloquent, or bright—
At every tone of music, at good and gentle things,
I feel a flutter in my heart like the fluttering of wings—
And I hear a low, wild warble, so strangely soft and sweet,
That with feelings inexpressible my pulse doth faster beat;
And I would not give the music that it sings unto my soul
For the diamonds of Golconda or a crowned queen's control

FRAGMENT.

From out the restless waters of the sea
The pale moon rises with her placid face—
So from the restless beating of my heart
A vision, fairer than the moon, steals up.
There were wild storms upon the sea last night!
Its waters had a sound of woe and madness—
So were there storms of passion in my heart
That had a sound of muttering and moans!
The sea is full of light and song this eve;
Its waves breathe music as they kiss the shore—
And so my heart is melted in its mood,
And murmurs e'er with tenderness and peace!

I think my heart is like the sea, my love,
Forever and forever like the sea!
Like it in terror, and in power and depth—
Like it in melody, and calm and light.
Now I will sing to thee as the waves sing;
And in the articulate music of the words,
That seek thy ear as ripples seek the shore,
Shall be defined the vision of my soul,
That rises from its restless, beating depths,
As the moon rises from the dimpling waves.

INA.

Dimples play at hide-and-seek
Upon Ina's crimson cheek—
Like the bud which wild-bees sip
Is her red and restless lip.
Soft brown tresses steal away
On her slender neck to play—
Lily white is each round arm—
Fairy is her girlish form.

Why is Ina blushing now?
Why so sobered her fair brow?
Why is her blue eyes thus hid
So demurely by the lid?
Why those orange flowers bright,
And that robe of spotless white?
We shall lose our village pride—
Ina is to be a bride!

Why is Ina silent now?
Why so pallid her white brow?

Why does the fringed lid thus lie
Moveless o'er her radiant eye?
Why so colorless her cheek?
Tell us why she does not speak—
Why comes not her gentle breath?
Ina is the bride of death!

Withered is the orange wreath—
Cold the forehead underneath!
Come, false bridegroom, who hath fled—
Come, and look upon the dead!
All your terrors naught avail—
Heart is still and bosom pale!
Wail and moan! you can not save—
Ina slumbers in the grave!

THE SILENT SHIP.

We were sitting in the starlight, by the gliding river's side—
He, a spirit pure and earnest—I, his sacred spirit-bride—
Sitting in the holy starlight falling from the jeweled sky
O'er the water just beneath us, flowing bright and silent by.
There was something dim and dreamy, and so solemn in the air,
And the earth was lying sweetly in her slumber still and fair;
And her breath had grown so quiet that a fold it did not stir
Of the green luxurious curtain drooping graceful over her.
Silent dew and silent starlight, silent earth and silent sky—
All was hushed save one faint murmur of the river flowing by—
And one low, dear tone of music, whispering in my thrilling ear,
Words so dreamlike in their beauty, that my soul could only hear;
Words so eloquent and gentle, that I never may forget—
They are ringing in sweet melody within my spirit yet!

In the dim, delicious silence, even the water fell asleep,
Looking bright, and pure, and placid, and immeasurably deep;
And subdued by this strange beauty, the communer by my side
Hushed his spiritual revealings, and sat voiceless by his bride.
How beautiful the stillness! this intense yet softened rest!
A perfect sense of happiness thrilled deep within each breast!
When as we watched the tremble of the starlight on the stream
From out the shadow of a curve all noiseless as a dream,
All slowly, softly, silently, all spirit-like and clear,
Gliding through the gently parting waves a vessel did appear.
We hushed our breath—we hushed our hearts—no echo of a sound
Came in through the dim loveliness, the solemn air around!
We gazed upon the silent ship—no sign of life was there,
Yet on it glided gracefully, all tall, and straight, and fair!
We saw the ripples break away and lose themselves in light,
As gently but unwaveringly it stole upon our sight;
We saw each slender spar and mast defined against the sky,
As slowly, softly, silently, it phantom-like went by.
A feeling of sublimity, which could not be expressed,
Sank heavy through the breathless hush upon each throbless breast—
A sense of something beautiful, yet almost to be feared,
As slowly, softly, silently, the strange ship disappeared.
"Sybil" was breathed upon my ear in one low thrilling tone,
And I felt the clasping of a hand grow tighter on my own.
It was enough—within our souls each felt that ship to be
An emblem of our spirit-love—our mingled destiny!
It seemed so like a hallowed spell, so like a lovely dream,
With lingering steps we turned away from the star-lighted stream;
Its beauty was so strange, and wild, and inexpressible,
That after many days had passed we found no words to tell
Our thoughts of dreamy loveliness and certainty it gave,
That thus our still, deep, spirit-love should glide upon life's wave.
Clouds now are o'er our silent ship, and not one starry gleam
Falls softly through the shadows that dim life's troubled stream;
There are storms, and clouds, and darkness, but I tremble not with fear,
For our ship will glide unshaken on till the stars again appear.

Such thoughts as these that silent ship within our souls awoke,
Are prophecies too sure and deep to be by darkness broke;
And whether there be storms or not, our spirits linked must be,
Till our bark is moored in safety in the far Eternity.

THERE IS A DREAM I CHERISH.

Youthful hearts will seek romances—
Youthful hearts will have their fancies;
And there is a dream I cherish
    That is with me all the day,
Of a grand old tree that springeth
Where its waving foliage flingeth
A soft shadow on the casement,
    Where I muse the hours away—
A soft shadow, weary never
    Of its light and shifting play.

This I dream—an angel spirit
Is forever hovering near it,
And within it and above it,
    With a mission from the sky!
For the old tree seems to love me,
As it waves its boughs above me
With a faint and gentle murmur,
    Or a low and saddened sigh;
For it seems to guard and cherish
    Even the wayward dreamer—I!

There's a whisper and a blessing
In the beautiful caressing
Of the leaves that stoop to kiss me

As I lean upon the sill;
And their murmur makes a feeling
That on earth hath no revealing,
But that sleepeth in my bosom
Mute and eloquent and still,
And their touch upon my forehead
Wakes a strangely pleasant thrill.

Where the topmost boughs are swinging,
And the waving leaves are singing
One low song of love forever
To the azure up on high,
Does my soul delight to hover,
With the cool leaves for a cover,
Resting in a swaying cradle,
Looking up into the sky!
With a motion soft as music
Swaying in the tree-top high!

O how blest is my wild spirit,
When no earthly thought is near it,
As it lies 'mid dreams and visions
In the arms of the old tree!
All the whispering leaflets bless it,
And the wild wind doth caress it,
And the soft and dreamy azure
Can my spirit only see;
And that seems to grow and deepen
Into strange infinity.

But there is a solemn hour
When the tree hath wilder power—
In the deep and starry midnight,
When I sit and watch the sky—
When the foliage moans and shivers,
And the starlight o'er it quivers,
And the shadows creep and tremble
O'er the casement where they lie—

Then the shadow and the whisper
Thrill my soul with mystery!

When the summer day is breaking,
And the earth is slowly waking—
When I throw the shutter open
To the morning fresh and fair,
And the spray doth bend before me,
Dashing shining dew-drops o'er me,
While the little leaves a-laughing,
Clap their bright hands in the air,
As the perfumed shower of jewels
Sparkles in my unbound hair.

Oh! I know no monarch olden
Wore a crown so brightly golden
Nor a robe so richly crimson
As the tree that loves me wore,
When the air was bright and dreaming,
And the heavens were blue and gleaming
In the glorious days of autumn,
That, alas, are now no more!
Then its murmur grew so mournful
As the sunny hours passed o'er.

Therefore, as my wayward spirit
Is forever blessed when near it,
As it seems to know and love me,
And is so beloved by me—
As its every whisper thrills me
And its midnight shadow fills me
With a thought of mystery—
Do I think some angel mission
Hovers ever in that tree!

LINES TO A POETESS.

Oh! poetess—young poetess!
  O lady fair and rare!
There is sweet starlight in thine eyes,
  Bright sunlight in thy hair;
There is soft music on thy lip,
  And radiance on thy brow;
Earth knoweth not a form of light
  More exquisite than thou.

I love to see the shadows start
  And deepen in thine eyes;
I love to watch their 'wildering wealth
  Of lashes slowly rise;
And mark the wild throb of thy heart
  Go flushing to thy cheek—
Thy restless lips' strange eloquence
  That scarcely needs to speak!

And oh! the glorious purity
  And pride of thy young face!
The murmur of the passionate words,
  The witchery of thy grace!
Most beautiful! most beautiful!
  How dare I love thee so,
Where love to such a heart as mine,
  Is surely only woe?

For love of mine for sympathy
  Too passionate is, and deep;
My lyre-strings when I touch them break,
  And when I sing I weep;
 mingle tears with starry thoughts,
  And sighs with wild sweet dreams,
And all my hopes go stilly by,
  Like blossoms down dark streams.

And thou—oh, thou! I sometimes fear
  Wilt learn that song of Fate,
That links with every happy note
  One sad and desolate;
For through the starlight of thine eyes
  I see the world it hides—
That by the fountains of its song
  A wild, wild spirit bides.

From where thou shinest in thy pride,
  I sadly sit apart,
And gather up thy smiles to glad
  My twilight gloom of heart.
I can not take from thee my eyes,
  These sad prophetic eyes,
O'er which I often wish the lids
  Might never, never rise.

I see thy glorious lip of red,
  Thy lip of love and pride,
And in its quiver read the thought
  Thy words perchance would hide;
I mark the eloquence of thy brow,
  The changing of thy face;
In the soft wreathing of thine arms
  I read thy spirit's grace.

O rare, pure, radiant poetess!
  Thy spell of life is love!
May he who winds it with his own
  Be watched by eyes above.
My thought of thee, oh! sweet young girl,
  With such deep care is fraught,
That words would surely turn to tears
  In mockery of that thought.

MIDNIGHT.

One by one, in slow succession,
  The twelve hours have floated by,
Circling, in a still procession,
  Round a glittering throne on high:
Handmaids to the solemn midnight
As she walketh up the sky.

With a motion slow and peerless,
  Up she glideth through the air,
Mutely perfect, smileless, tearless,
  Hushed, and wonderfully fair—
Pausing, in her quiet splendor,
Where her twelve attendants are.

All the stars their brows uncover,
  All the breezes die away,
All the hours which round her hover
  Stand in dim and mute array;
For the midnight, pure and placid,
Kneeleth on her throne to pray.

Grand beyond the power of telling
  Is the midnight in her prayer—
All sublimity has dwelling
  On her brow serenely fair;—
Brighter than the crown of jewels
Bound upon her raven hair.

She is asking for a blessing
  On the earth that dreams below,
And the leaves, their boughs caressing,
  Cease their waving to and fro—
And the murmuring, trilling streamlet
Seems to sing more soft and slow.

Her pure eyes are upward beaming,
  And her pale hands folded lie—
Oh! how beautiful this seeming
  Of the queen of all the sky,
Meekly asking, 'mid her glory,
From the greater power on high.

In her dim and holy presence
  The still world has grown more still,
And soft silence' subtile essence
  Seems the breathless air to fill,
Till the hushed heart of creation
Scarcely dares with awe to thrill.

In serene, subduing splendor,
  When her time of prayer has flown,
Through the circle that attend her,
  She descendeth from her throne—
Gliding westward from the zenith,
As they follow, one by one.

All the stars their faces cover,
  All the flowers droop with tears,
And the breezes round them hover
  With a whispered tale of fears,
As the Midnight Queen retireth,
And the King of Day appears.

Were I but a star in heaven,
  Or a little flower, alone,
I would worship, every even,
  The sweet midnight on her throne;
But a worship yet more perfect
Hath the living spirit known.

THE SPIRIT OF MY SONG.

Tell me—have you ever met her—
 Met the spirit of my song—
Have her wave-like footsteps glided
 Through the city's worldly throng?
You will know her by a wreath,
 Woven all of starry light,
That is lying 'mid her hair—
 Braided hair as dark as night.

A short band of radiant summers
 Is upon her forehead laid,
Twining half in golden sunlight,
 Keeping half in dreamy shade;
Five white fingers clasp a lyre,
 Five its silvery strings awake,
And bewildering to the soul
 Is the music that they make.

Though her glances sleep like shadows
 'Neath each falling, silken lash,
Yet at aught that wakes resentment,
 They magnificently flash.
Though you loved such dewy dream-light,
 And such glances of sweet surprise,
You could never bear the scorn
 Of these proud and brilliant eyes.

There's a sweet and winning curving
 In her bright lip's crimson hue,
And a glittering tint of roses
 From her soft cheek gleaming through;
Do you think that you have met her?
 She is young and pure and fair,
And she wears a wreath of starlight
 In her braided ebon hair.

Often at her feet I'm sitting,
With my head upon her knee,
While she tells me dreams of beauty
In low words of melody;
And when my unskillful fingers
Strive her silvery lyre to wake,
She will smooth my tresses, smiling
At the discord which I make.

But of late days I have missed her—
The bright being of my love—
And perchance she's stolen pinions,
And has floated up above.
Tell me—have you ever met her—
Met the spirit of my song—
Have her wave-like footsteps glided
Through the city's worldly throng?

THE DREAMER.

A DREAMER rose from her quiet sleep
To look out upon the night,
And the light that fell from the shining sky
Ne'er fell on a maid more bright:
For the youthful form in those robes of snow
Was full of a breathing grace,
And fashioned in perfect loveliness
Was the beauty of her face.
In the rosy palm of her dimpled hand
One red cheek nestling lay,
And smiles stole out from her coral lips
With that lily hand to play;

The thick, dark lashes were lifted up
  To a brow as pure as snow,
And dark, and soft, and beautiful
  Were the eyes that shone below;
They were dark, and soft, and beautiful,
  And full of a dewy light,
And stars like those in the skies were there,
  But a hundred times more bright.

The young moon seemed like a boat of pearl,
  With a soft light shining through,
To pilot the stars on their way through heaven,
  O'er a sea of pathless blue;
And the air was full of melody—
  For the rustle of leafy trees,
And the dreamy murmur of dimpled waves
  Stole away on the winged breeze;
And the earth slept sweet in her night attire,
  Bejeweled with perfumed dew,
And 'broidered o'er with flowers and leaves,
  And buds of many a hue.

The dreamer gazed on this loveliness
  Till her cheek was one crimson glow,
And the life in her heart throbbed hurriedly,
  And her breath came quick and low;
And those eyes, so dreamy, and soft, and sweet,
  And so full of dewy light,
Forgot their calm, clear, spirit-look,
  And grew dark, wild, and bright;
A beauty too dazzling for that of earth
  Stole over her upturned face,
And it seemed that the living soul breathed out
  From the lines in that form of grace;
Her lips were parted and tremulous,
  And when at length she spoke,
Like the music of tinkling water-drops,
  The words from her red lips broke;

For her tones were fashioned of music's tones,
And her breath was but a lyre,
That faintly echoed the melody
Of the dreamer's thoughts of fire:

"I knew, I knew that it thus would be—
To-night I shall read my destiny!
The world may smile, for I know it deems
These thoughts of mine are but idle dreams;
But I feel, I know, that it must be so!
There are spirits around, above, below—
And now, in the glorious time of night,
They fill the earth with their presence bright.
I see them now with their radiant wings,
Flitting about among beautiful things;
Flitting through sky, and earth, and air,
Leaving new loveliness everywhere.
They give to the flowers their delicate hue,
And place a gem in each drop of dew;
I see them bring on their pinions fair,
The starlight down through the dreamy air.
'Tis the wave of their wings that startles the breeze
That murmurs so low in the shadowy trees;
They sail on the waves of the shining lake,
And their motions a rippling melody make;
They breathe on the air their soft perfumes,
And they sleep in the blossoms with folded plumes;
They leave their robes for the lily-flower,
And the blush on their cheek is the rose's dower;
And every star has its forehead fair
Bound round with a tress of their shining hair;
Forever and ever they flit around,
Filling the earth with a mystic sound;
And they say strange musical words to me,
Till my soul is bewildered with melody.
They whispered, last night, that this hour I
Should read my fate on the evening sky;
That the shining stars would reveal to me

The book of the dreamer's destiny.
I hear them now! and they bid me look
On the charmed page of this mystic book!
Each star has changed to a word of light—
And this is the fate that I read to-night:

"'Beautiful dreamer! 'tis but for thee
To know of earth's hidden mystery;
To thee alone is it given to see
The spell of our secret ministry.
Thou art our chosen! before whose eyes
This beautiful world like a clear page lies;
Each bud and flower doth to thee possess
A new and a wonderful loveliness—
And the flutter of one green leaf will fill
Thy soul with a quick, low, quivering thrill;
And even the breath that is given to thee
Is fraught with a witching melody,
Till even the ringing of dropping rain
Doth sound to thee like a music-strain.
These are the gifts which to thee belong,
Thou chosen one of the spirit-throng!
But the world is dark, and it can not know
Of these priceless treasures which we bestow.
We have watched it well, when it coldly smiled
At the beautiful dreams of our gifted child;
And when it has listened, and looked, and heard,
Entranced by the charm of thine every word,
We have seen its wonder and awed surprise
Concealed by the scorn of its envious eyes;
And we know that thy being, so frail and fair,
Will wither away in the poisoned air;
And thy golden lyre be crushed by the weight
Of the cold, rude fingers of bitter hate!
We know that on earth there never lives
The earnest love that thy spirit gives,
And we sorrow now that we gave to thee
Those gifts which on earth bring misery;

But we love thee still! and if thou wilt come,
We will bear thee to heaven—thy own bright home!' "

She had read her fate! "Well, be it so!"
Was her soft reply; as with head bent low
On her folded hands, and her raven hair
Forming a pall for that form so fair,
And the long, dark lashes down-drooping meek,
To the pale, and pearly, and smiling cheek:
With these murmured words her spirit fled—
And the beautiful dreamer of earth was dead!

LINES.

My soul has been sleeping
In darkness too long,
Forgetful of music,
Of sunlight, and song!
It has stilled its wild warbles,
And folded its wings,
And slumbered all dreamless
'Mid beautiful things.

The soft, holy starlight
Has over it crept,
Nor won by its beauty
The spirit that slept:
Around it has floated
A thousand perfumes—
Their breath never stirring
Its close folded plumes.

And music most thrilling—
So wild and so deep—
Had no power to awaken
My soul from its sleep!
Lid-shadowed its visions—
Lip-stilled its low tone—
From its brow was the beauty
Of earnest thought flown.

The lyre which its fingers
Unconsciously held,
No more 'neath those fingers
With melody swelled.
The slumber is broken—
The darkness is past!
My soul has awakened
To true life at last!

Its pulses quick thrilling
At every thing bright,
And its plumes all a-quiver
With startled delight!
Lids parted to starlight,
Lips parted to song,
While around it bright fancies,
Like starry lights, throng!

'Neath its tremulous fingers
The lyre swells sweet,
With a tone too bewitching
For lips to repeat.
Keep thrilling, keep thrilling,
And waving thy wings!
God made thee to glory
In beautiful things.

Now never, oh! never,
Shall slumber enchain

The free-bounding pulse
  Of my spirit again.
It hath wakened exulting
  In life, love, and power;
Soul-life is immortal—
  Thank God for the dower!

TO WILLIAM CULLEN BRYANT.

A low, soft voice, of sweetest singing,
  Swells out upon the evening breeze,
And all the air around seems ringing
  With its fine floating harmonies.
From yonder lattice comes the breathing
  Of that sad, sweet, and spiritual song,
Where graceful vines are thickly wreathing,
  And dewy roses clustering throng.

I see a face, like starlight shining,
  Glance out into the dewy night;
I see a white arm softly twining
  Around a column gray and light,
I see her dark eyes, upward throwing
  Their mournful, wild, impassioned sight;—
I see her wild hair, backward flowing
  Around a young form sweetly slight;

I see her red lips deeply flushing,
  And trembling with the liquid trill
Of music from her bosom gushing,
  That all the starry air doth fill;

I hear the melody, and wonder
  How all the roses sparkle still,
And all the shadows sleeping under,
  Lie quiet on the soulless sill.

Her song is scarce of earthly feeling,
  Yet something of an earthly love;
Her deep tones still forever stealing
  Their wildest cadence from above;
Just as her eyes, with their long lashes
  Laid backward to her forehead high,
Drink down their softest, saddest flashes
  From the sweet starlight of the sky.

I know the singer is immortal,
  Yet earthly while on earth she sighs;
But soon as opes their radiant portal,
  That moment will she reach the skies!
That grand, deep strain, as still I hear it,
  And see that vision pure and rare,
I know it is thine own song-spirit
  That chants unto the 'tranced air!

There is no harp whose grandest pealing
  Could flatter this pure bride of thine—
Yet can I choose one flower of feeling
  And lay it softly on her shrine.
With gentle reverence I am kneeling
  In her rare presence, proud and sweet,
While the bright starlight round me stealing,
  Like me, bends down to kiss her feet.

A SUMMER STORM.

Hear the low wailing blast of the heralding breeze
Rise, rushing and swelling, above the bowed trees!
While, with shadowing wings, creeping o'er the blue skies,
Like hovering ravens the mighty clouds rise,
As swiftly and surely they gather and spread!
No sunlight—no ether—the storm is o'erhead!
Now! loose thy dark tresses and wave thy white wand!
Be ready, young Sybil, the storm is at hand!
Hush, hush, heart, thy beating—the world is so still
You would break the awed silence by even one thrill.
'Tis the pause in the tempest, the moment of rest,
When the storm-spirit looseth the sword 'neath his breast.
Oh! spirit majestic; oh! spirit of might!
With your glittering sword and your armor of night;
I feel not a fear, by thy wildness though awed,
For thy Maker is mine; we were fashioned by God!
Ha! from thy strong hand is a thunderbolt hurled!
There's a gleam on the forest, a flash o'er the world—
Then a mutter, a rumble, a crash through the sky,
As the voice of thine anger rolls sternly on high;
And the silence shrinks back, and the giant trees creak
'Neath the weight of the breath that comes down with a shriek—
Then the clatter of hail from thy wings shaken down,
As darker and fiercer is growing thy frown!
Till mingling together in tumult most grand
Leap the weapons of battle from out thy right hand,
Fierce flashing, wild crashing—the rush of the blast,
And the clatter of hail falling fast and more fast.
O spirit—storm-spirit! misuse not thy power!
The earth does not mock thee nor shrink in this hour,
But she beareth thy wrath not to fear or deride—
Then cease thy vain battle, dark spirit of pride!
There is something can conquer thine anger with love—
'Tis the smile of the day-god who rideth above.

He has parted thy banners to gaze on the world—
How gracefully rolling those banners are furled.
Ah! loosen thine armor and fold thy black wings—
Thou never canst war with the glory he brings;
His smile is upon thee and over thee now,
And the frowning hath vanished from off thy wild brow;
Thy black robes grow crimson, thy pinions are gold,
The embrace of the sun round thy dark form doth fold.
What! melted to weeping? O beautiful sight!
The storm-spirit weeping sweet tears of delight!
And see, those soft tears dropping down from on high,
How they glitter and gleam through the depths of the sky.
O beautiful wonder! most charming surprise!
The day-god hath caught them far up in the skies,
And woven them sparkling like diamonds bright,
In a crown of such splendor as 'wilders the sight,
And bound them thus rare on the storm-spirit's brow;
If in anger majestic how eloquent now!
The battle is ended—the victory was love;
How glorious the triumph that glitters above,
As he leadeth the spirit, subdued yet how fair,
Through the splendor he makes in the soft swelling air.
The sun and storm-spirit together will rest—
Together they're seeking their home in the west;
Together in glory, with banner half furled,
They have smiled their farewell to the beautiful world,
And went down in their splendor together to sleep,
'Neath the glittering waves of the welcoming deep.
Now, Sybil, young Sybil, thank God he hath made
A picture thus lovely with glitter and shade,
To be hung in the temple where memory dwells,
And her lyre ever thrilling with blissfulness swells.
And lo! as I kneel 'mid the fragrance and dew,
A soft star the twilight steps tremblingly through,
And kisses my forehead and smiles in my eyes,
As she stealeth my prayer to her home in the skies!

STARLIGHT.

There were startles in my slumber and I had uneasy dreams,
And the night of sleep was broken with wild, fitful, feverish gleams;
For my heart was almost broken ere my pillow I had sought;
And my soul was almost maddened with such sorrow was it fraught.
A mocking, taunting image filled my sleep with bitter pain,
Telling it of past enchantment that should never be again,
When a sudden, silent presence o'er my pillow softly broke—
Calm, subdued, and comprehending, then my mournful soul awoke.
I knew by intuition that a spirit hovered near,
And I lay in placid wonder but without a thrill of fear.
Through the shadows of the roses with their perfume and their dew,
By the open casement bending came the silent spirit through;
And its feet were on my pillow, silver feet they were and bright,
And its eyes were bent upon me with a soft, sweet, solemn light.
Stiller than the stillest midnight gazed it down into my eyes,
And the wherefore of its presence filled me with a mute surprise.
The memory of my sorrow, my wild and withering woe,
And the visions of my slumber that had flitted to and fro,
Made me think the still, white spirit came to bring me some relief
From the bitterness of anguish and the hopelessness of grief.
Through the awe that overcame me my despairing soul out-broke,
And to the still, deep vision with eagerness I spoke:
"Starlight! rare and radiant starlight! wherefore did you leave your home
'Mid the jewels and the azure of yon grand and glittering dome?
Did you know my heart was broken—did you know my fate was crossed?
Did you come to teach the mystery of regaining what is lost?
Did you come to soothe my mourning and to cool my fevered brain,
And to whisper of life's sweetness to my aching heart again?
O spirit! sweet, pale spirit! he who loved me and caressed,
With his kiss upon my forehead and my cheek upon his breast—
Him to whom I gave the reverence and the trusting of a child,
With the earnest love of woman, deep and passionate and wild—

All the madness and the power and the fervor of my soul—
Its wild and burning eloquence gushing out without control—
We have parted in deep bitterness, have used the words of scorn,
Have torn the roses of our love and clasped the cruel thorn—
Have mocked at bygone sweetness and smiled at what we lost,
And our words have fell in coldness as the winter spray drops frost.
Pale starlight! did you seek me from your chamber up in heaven,
To tell me how to win again the jewels I have given?
Have you no draught of Lethe? no magic did you bring,
To make the roses blossom and to heal the bitter sting?"
But the spirit yet was silent and its robes grew paler still,
And it gazed upon me with a gaze that made my bosom thrill;
Its eyes were sad and solemn and it seemed to mock my grief,
And to pitiless reproach me that my sorrow sought relief.
"Starlight!" pleaded I in anguish, "oh, sweet starlight, hear my prayer—
From my heart so sad and weary take away this weight of care.
Do you think that we should suffer all the anguish we incurred
When we taunted true affection with a cold and stinging word?
Have you learned no gentle pity from the angels up above?
Do you not know the waywardness of wildly passionate love?
Tell me if our injured spirits shall forget the hapless past,
Or if all will be forgiven and our souls be blent at last."
But the pallid vision hovered with no answer 'round my bed,
And its silver footsteps trembled on the pillow 'neath my head.
A solemn awe was o'er it that my mad soul could not brook—
I could not bear the agony of meeting its mute look.
"Starlight! mocking starlight!" pleaded I, "away! away!
On the anguish past endurance bring no more of grief to lay!
Leave me—leave me to my mourning! take away your solemn eyes!
Take back your taunting radiance to yonder silent skies!
I knew the hollow-heartedness of earthly forms of love—
Why came you to destroy the hope of sympathy above?"
But the pale, cold, silver starlight would not let me sink to rest,
But crept closer, till its fingers lay like ice upon my breast;
And I moaned in helpless agony and turned my face away,
And with my hand upon my eyes I waited for the day.

PLEADINGS.

A SHADOW has lain on my soul all day—
Sunlight and gladness have staid away.
Heavy and cold has the shadow prest
Like palpable darkness upon my breast;
Sadness and silence are in our room,
Better befitting my spirit's gloom—
Sister! sweet sister! oh, come away,
From the music wild and the dancers gay!

Who twined these roses amid my hair?
Who decked my form in these robings fair?
Are they befitting the heart they fold?
My cheek is pale and my lip is cold!
The lamps and flowers too brilliant seem,
They 'wilder my sight like a mocking dream—
Sister! sweet sister! oh, come away,
From the music wild and the dancers gay!

Seeks *he* ever such revels now?
He sits 'neath the stars with a pale, stern brow,
And his soul grows wild that our perfect trust
Lies shivered and dark in the mourning dust;
And his calm lip curls with a bitter scorn
At the love and faith which are earthly born—
Sister! sweet sister! oh, come away,
From the music wild and the dancers gay!

I can not smile at each merry glance—
I move in a dream through the gliding dance—
My thought has flown to the starlight dim
That hovers with silver step near him.
Never! oh, never! shall we again
Soothe from each other the throb of pain—

Sister! sweet sister! oh, come away,
From the music wild and the dancers gay!

A shadow has lain on my soul all day—
Vainly I whisper it, "Flee away!"
Chill and heavy, and silent and slow,
It sinks more dark o'er the pale, still woe
That fainting lies in my spirit's gloom,
Mocked by this light and this sweet perfume—
Sister! sweet sister! oh, come away,
From the music wild and the dancers gay!

I've plead with the shadow to leave my breast!
I've striven to banish my soul's unrest!
But I only hear in the music's tone
A solemn sound, like a smothered moan,
And I only see where the lamp-light lies,
The mournful gaze of those proud, sad eyes—
Sister! sweet sister! oh, come away,
From the music wild and the dancers gay!

THE POET'S DECLARATION.

Twilight shadows gathering 'round me,
  Firelight flickering on the wall,
With their waving drapery bound me—
  Bound me and the quaint old hall—
Quaint old hall where I sat dreaming
  Idly in an antique chair,
  Watching the fitful firelight rare!
Spiritual visitors sought and found me
  Musing 'mid the drapery there.

Every time that the shadows shifted
  Then would the drapery rise and fall—
Gliding in when the curtains lifted,
  Visions came at my fanciful call—
Faint, fair visions, wonderful spirits,
  Came and looked into my eyes
  Too calm to waken a soft surprise—
Silent their steps as the light that rifted
  The dim sweet that around them lies.

Was I afraid when my tinkling fancies
  Called these forms to my grand old chair?
Ah, no! eager for quaint romances,
  Awe and terror forgotten were.
Sitting calm as a stately emperor,
  After the silvery summons rung
  Waited I till the visitants sprung
With steps like those when a star-beam dances,
  Through where the rifted drapery hung.

Faint, faint forms and sweet, sweet faces
  Hovered about in the dreamy light,
Dimly embodying eloquent graces,
  Floating tresses and mantles bright.
And I will tell you—love, will you listen?
  Of one visitant dear and fair
  Who came glidingly to my chair—
Hers was the purest of all pure faces,
  Wild and dark was her unbound hair.

Rare young vision! that dark hair flowing
  Wound on the air like the wing of a bird;
Sweet was her cheek with its crimson glowing—
  Sweet was her voice with its one wild word—
One wild word that she murmured ever—
  One low, clear, continued word,
  Like a tinkling stream through shadows heard,
Over her lip in music flowing!
  "Love!" dear, "love," was the whispered word.

Closer and closer her white robe fluttered
  Through the dim drapery the twilight made—
Softer and lower the word that she uttered—
  Over my forehead her faint breath played!
Her faint breath played and her slender fingers
  Lifted aside my careless hair
  With a touch as soft as a touch of air;
And she kissed my brow as I wondering muttered,
  "Love?" ay, "love," answered young lips rare.

One white arm with a way caressing
  Lay like a wreath around my hair;
Close to mine was her warm cheek pressing,
  Close in mine lay her fingers fair.
The hours went by and the firelight flickered,
  Yet the sweet dream still breathed on me
  Till my soul was flooded with ecstasy;
And her voice was soft as an angel's blessing!
  All winter I wondered what this might be.

But ah! sweet spring! one eve reclining
  'Mid crimson flowers and fragrant air,
The wonder ceased! before me shining
  I saw that face and fluttering hair!
My heart throbbed up with wild emotion
  And *her* cheek flushed a deeper hue,
  Till she looked so like—so like—like *you!*
For the word she uttered I'm weary pining—
  Dearest, now may the dream come true?

THE DEAD MOTHER.

SWEET mother! thou art dead! I feel it now;
Thy pallid face once oh! so sweet and fair—
The death-dew damp upon thy pale, cold brow
So strangely white beneath its parted hair—
The curtained eye from whence all light hath fled,
The still, drooped lid—oh, mother! thou art dead!

Dear mother! speak to me! it is thy boy
Who calls so wildly on thy name the while:
One little word would bring such raptured joy!
Thou dost not speak—thou dost not even smile.
Upon thy moveless lip there is no breath—
It does not even quiver—this is death!

Oh, mother! look on me! The dark still fringe
Rests all too heavy on thy ashy cheek,
On which the sleeping blood has left no tinge,
And the love-smile will never, never speak.
Thou wilt not look on me—not let one gleam
Of deep affection from thy closed eyes beam.

Dear mother! thou art cold—thy hand is chill—
It answers not the pressure of my own—
Thy heart knows no emotion—feels no chill—
Hushed on thy lip is its low, loving tone;
The folded linen motionless doth rest
In snowy whiteness on thy chilly breast.

I had a dream last night—I was a child—
Thy fingers toyed amid my curls, and thou
Bent fondly over me and sweetly smiled,
Leaving a mother's kiss upon my brow;
I heard thy voice and saw thy dear eyes beam—
Alas! alas! that it should be a dream!

Oh, mother! *can* it be that thou art gone?
  That I must live and yet not have thee near?—
That I must suffer and still on,
  Apart from her to my lone heart most dear?
My brain grows dizzy and my brow doth ache—
My weary, weary heart will surely break!

Sweet mother! they have closed the coffin-lid,
  And shut thee up within its awful gloom,
And thy dear form forever now is hid,
  And left to moulder in the damp, dark tomb.
Away with tears! the mockery of grief!
My maddened sorrow findeth no relief!

Dear mother! I do know, if thou wert here,
  That thou wouldst chide the wildness of my woe;
And so no sign of suffering shall appear—
  I'll hush the heart-strings that are quivering so—
Thinking thy spirit hovers 'round me still,
I will be calm—will quiet each sad thrill.

HUMILITY.

There's a quaint and quiet comer
  In my soul hath dwelt all day,
With her white hands softly folded,
  And her robe of sober gray—
But in vain have brighter dwellers
  Sought to frighten her away.

Once to-day, a radiant sparkler,
  With a face of roguish glee,
Glided up, and asked demurely

What the comer's name might be?
And she raised her eyes and answered,
Low and soft, "Humility."

And the little dancer wondered
That she had such lovely eyes,
And almost wished *her* crimson lips
Could make such sweet replies;
Yet such a face with such a dress
Still filled her with surprise.

And she scorned the quiet comer
With the brown and braided hair,
For her own flowed down in ringlets,
And was looped with flowers fair,
And she did not fancy sober robes
When hers with gems shone rare.

So no one sought the stranger
With the sweet head bowed so low—
With the fair and placid forehead,
And the hands as white as snow;
But she smiled to be neglected
As the rest passed to and fro.

But the evening now is coming
When my soul shuts up its halls,
And the silvery voice of music
To the evening worship calls
All the thousand flitting dwellers
That have been within its walls.

The dancing and the singing ones
Are weary of their play;
They come with lingering footsteps
And tones no longer gay,
And gather sad and silently
In mute and tired array.

And some, the dark and restless ones,
  Have wandered off and died,
And many grand and lofty ones
  Have yielded up their pride;—
With broken wings and broken lutes
  They gather side by side.

And now the meek-browed stranger,
  With the robe of pensive gray,
With a face of holy calmness
  Bends quietly to pray;
And from her form the mantle
  Of meekness falls away;

And underneath is flowing
  A robe like sunset fair,
And, her golden wings unfolding,
  She floats into the air!
And now I know I've "*entertained*
  An angel unaware!"

DEATH AT MIDNIGHT.

Why have I started from my dreams?
The soft, sweet starlight round me gleams,
A tinkling sound of silver streams
    Doth faintly sing and sigh;
The wind doth come like fingers fair,
And from my forehead lift my hair,
And calmly through the swelling air
    The stars look from the sky.
This is my last, last living sleep!

I do not wake to vigils keep,
Nor yet to struggle or to weep—
    I wake to pray and die.

My mother slumbers with no fear,
And all these cherished ones and dear,
Undreaming what is passing here,
    Sleep softly till the light.
I wonder if before this day,
Ever, like me, so young and gay,
In loneliness has passed away
    A spirit in the night,
With no one by, her lips to press,
To give and take the last caress,
To speak of heaven, to pray, to bless,
    And tell of angels bright?

So softly does my pulse grow still,
So sweetly does my faint heart thrill,
There is no terror in the chill
    That creeps into my breast.
My wild, high spirit longs to go,
It was so restless here below—
Sweet visions hover to and fro—
    This is a pleasant rest!
Yet half I wish the world had heard
The grand, rare music that hath stirred,
Unspoken yet by song or word,
    The throbbings of my breast.

I wonder if my friends will weep,
When, waking from their quiet sleep,
They find *my* slumber is the deep,
    Deep slumber of the grave!
That all their tenderness and care,
And many a wild and anxious prayer,
And all *his* desolate despair
    My young life may not save—

That there is no more soul in me
Than there is light within the sea
When midnight shroudeth silently
The still and shadowed wave.

Sweet Heaven! be merciful to all
When on Thy name they wailing call,
And do not let my shadow fall
Upon one sunny way;
Let no one yearn, with mourning bowed,
To rest within the cold, fair shroud,
That lies as lies a waving cloud
Around my pale, still clay.
Sweet, solemn music, soft and slow—
The starry air doth 'round me flow—
The curtain waveth to and fro—
They call my soul away!

It is a beautiful thing to die!
To pass away while calm I lie
With eyes uplifted to the sky
And only stars to see!
When all my soul was in a storm,
And sorrow shook my suffering form,
And bitter woes chilled yearnings warm,
Death! I have pined for thee
To still my pulse—and yet! oh, yet!
Strange, that I could this hour forget
How sweet was life since *we two* met—
Since soul and soul met we!

How sweet! since with uplifted eyes
We sat beneath the sapphire skies—
While hand in hand all warmly lies—
And bosoms softly beat—
With oh! such rare and spiritual thought,
To our hushed souls by evening brought,

While lips, with love's low eloquence fraught,
    Ran o'er with murmurs sweet.
Yet even his love, his words, his kiss,
Once wild, intense, and fervid bliss,
I can resign when death like this
    Comes pleading to my feet.

I see such waving arms and hair—
Such white robes fluttering on the air—
Such starry eyes and foreheads fair
    Come glistening 'round my head!
The drapery waveth soft and low,
The shadows creep and quiver so,
And perfumed roses come and go
    'Mid dew on roses shed—
And like a visible silver stream
That melts to an invisible dream,
Soft waves of music swell and gleam
    And float around my bed.

I faint—I die—oh, lover dear—
Oh! fond ones that are slumbering near,
You could not weep one mournful tear
    Above my shrouded clay,
If you could list this melody,
These radiant angels could you see,
And know with what soft ecstasy
    I fainted slow away;
You would dread, nor weep, nor fear
The glory and the rapture here—
Farewell—farewell! oh, sleepers dear!
    In heaven for all I'll pray.

This perfume takes away my breath!
This music swells my form beneath,
And bears me on the waves of death—
    So softly do I lie.

Sweet spirits—stars—deep angel eyes
That smile upon me through the skies—
Oh, floating sounds that 'round me rise
And bear me high—more high!
Bewildered heart—so still—so still—
My blissful spirit can not thrill—
I faint—sweet Heaven, be with me still—
float—I faint—I die.

ENDURANCE.

THE deepest mourning that the human heart
Can ache with and not break, is mine to-night.
It is not softened grief, so beautiful;
It does not lay a thin and wasted hand
Upon the plaintive strings of a sweet lyre,
And with its eyes upraised chant saddened hymns!
Nor does it beat with the quick agony
That breaks the iron bars of reason down,
And from mind's cage flies with wild, burning wings,
Whose quivering motions set themselves on fire
Until they perish in their fearful flight.
It is not madness! and it is not grief!
But deep, abiding, and black, solemn woe
That presses with a heavy, heavy hand
Upon my bosom, till no life is there—
Nor even the desolate music of despair—
Nor the grand funeral gloom of coffined sleep—
Nor the disheveled dress of sorrow pale.
It is not life—and yet it is not death!
But oh! as if my heart lay beating thick
And throbbing slowly in its muffled gloom,

Apart, alone, beneath the damp, dark earth,
A thousand, thousand feet in buried life!
Who can conceive such close, oppressive woe—
Such helpless, hopeless, heavy agony?
My heart—my heart! buried alive! so far
From love and light, and music and the stars!
How fearfully and slowly it beats up,
To make itself a little room to throb,
To pant, to gasp, within its terrible grave!
How heavily the cold weight presses down!
How shall I save my heart—once eloquent heart—
That sung and bounded in the light of joy?
The days to me will be like centuries!
Endure—endure—endure the fearful fate
That prisons up within its horrible gloom
The soul that would grow wild, if it had room!
Say, shall I crush my writhing lip between
The teeth that grate and clench themselves in pain?
Say, shall I wring my twining hands till they
Have crushed their quivering fingers in their clasp,
And smite my forehead on the chilly wall,
And start and rise, and shriek and pace my room
With steps as if the floor were red-hot iron?
Oh, no, no, no! I have no such relief!
I would that I *could* mourn as others mourn!
Come madness, with your fearful phantasies!
Come wailing song, come tears, come frantic grief!
Come every mocking shape of fearfulness—
Come terror and sharp pain—come any thing!
Except this suffocating, throbbing woe—
This close, oppressive, endless misery!
Would I could die! but my heart dieth not;
It is as if a thousand years from now,
Strong, sinewy hands should toil, and toil, and toil,
Lifting up, one by one, cold, heavy stones,
And mouldy earths, and ruins of the past,
Till deep below, pressed round by chilly soil,
They found my heart—yet beating—beating still,

Slowly and sullenly, against the weight
Of darkness and of damp that built it up
So deep, and close, and terrible a grave.
Endure! that word is to me like the star
That seems so insignificant to the eye
Of him who looks but does not comprehend—
Yet to the one who reads its mystery,
Is full of life and pain and centuries—
Ay! of eternity and soul and God!
The golden stars once to my happy eyes
Were burning thoughts of bliss and eloquence;
But now they fashion that one word—endure!
And every sullen pulse of my slow heart
Mutters and murmurs o'er the endless word.
I press my cold hands over it and plead
And say, hush—hush, my heart! my heart, be still!
Yet with a solemn throbbing it keeps on.
Oh! if I could but free this prisoned pain,
And expiate endurance in one shriek,
Methinks the terrified night at that wild shriek
Would faint into the arms of the pale shades
That from all haunted ruins and deep graves
Would rush and startle, moan and die away!
The miners toil not down through fearful pits
As my hopes toil to reach my buried heart—
Yet find it not, and perish while they toil.
Yet this sad, aching thing, in days gone by,
Was like a rose-tree in a summer-clime—
All full of singing birds and perfume sweet,
And fresh white tears dropped by the sparkling stars.
Now—oh, now! it weeps not, sings not, loves not!
But from its grave there comes a hollow sound—
A gasping, and a throbbing, and a moan—
Repeating o'er and o'er, endure—endure!
And why and wherefore is this living grave
I know not; this I know—my happy heart
Was full of bliss, and tenderness, and music,
When a dark woe came up and breathed on it,

Till with a sigh it fainted in my breast.
Despair said hurriedly, "'Tis dead—'tis dead!"
And while my young joys gathered 'round and wept,
Sad sorrow sang the solemn funeral hymn—
And thus they buried it—and now it wakes
To gasp forever in its terrible grave.
Heaven's great magnificence and earth's delight—
All splendor, grandeur, sunshine, and sweet hopes—
All revelations of the wonderful—
All storms of terror and all calms of joy,
Are hid from it forever—evermore!
But in its grave are hidden these two things—
Endurance and Eternity.

THE WINDS.

A LOVELY girl leaned from an open casement.
She was, of all, the most surpassing fair—
For surely nothing we regard as so
Was like to her in perfectness of fairness,
Just like the brightness of succeeding waves
That lose themselves in shade and gleam again;
The golden river of her shining hair
Flowed round the beauty of her youthful form—
That shone from out that stream of glorious hair,
Like a sweet island in a southern clime,
Smiling amid its rippling waves of gold.
There was a blended beauty in her face,
Of all the starry lights that burn in heaven,
And all the tinted flowers that glow on earth.
Her white young forehead, shadowed by her hair,
Had a soft, spiritual development,
Made earthly only by its passionate brows;

And 'neath them shone those soft out-glancing eyes—
Those large, pure, loving eyes—those fathomless eyes—
Those bright and blue, those fringed and shaded eyes!
Her sweetly curved and eloquent red lips
Were parted in the eagerness of joy!
A faint, fresh color wavered in her cheek,
As if it knew not or to stay or go;
There was a smile in that bright glance of hers,
As if she looked for flowers—on that red lip,
As if it fain would call the singing-birds—
And that uncertain glow upon her cheek,
Said—"Ah, they are—they are not—are they come?"
It was a young Spring day, balmy and fresh,
And the warm wind came to her, telling tales
How the green grass was creeping from the earth,
And the bright buds were glowing in the dell—
And as she felt its breath, so full of sweets,
She wondered if the violets had come;
And lingered at the casement, thrilled and blessed
By the soft touches of the balmy wind,
With a soft fluttering motion, from her arms,
Her bosom, and her girdle, floated back
The airy muslin of her simple robe.
She wore no jewels and no snowy pearls—
They would have shown like baubles upon *her*—
So delicate, so refined her loveliness;
And all the golden waves upon her neck,
Glittered the more the wind came up,
And kissed her beautiful throat in loving joy;
Ah! that uncertain joy and eagerness!
That asking, bright'ning glance and flushing cheek!
That trembling eloquence of the glad lip!
This young Spring wind so full of sweets to come—
So full of buds that sometimes would be flowers
What was this young Spring wind that breathed such tales?

Again—the maiden sat within her bower!
Her little snow-soft hands, in placid rest,

Lay folded motionless within her lap;
The light of dreams lay like a silver vail,
Over and all around her glowing form—
Softening the splendor of her radiance;
Her still, soft, sapphire eyes were downward cast,
To hide the little blisses floating round
In the clear liquid of their azure depths,
While, with a tremulous and golden gleam,
The long, bright lashes drooped above those eyes.
A warm, sweet, loving glow was on the lip
That smiled and murmured with her rosy dreams;
And the once wavering flush upon her cheek,
Had deepened to the richness of content.
There was deep meaning on her brilliant brow—
So placid yet so passionate its repose;
Oh! beautiful was she, and soft her dreams!
The while she mused the soft south wind stole up,
And stirred the drapery of her still form;
It was not damp with violets—but rich
With roses, and magnolias, and carnations,
And lilies spotless as her youthful brow.
This Summer wind, so heavy with perfume,
The lady breathed in with her smiling lips,
And still, as if no offering was meet
For one so glorious and so fair as her,
It brought up rarer fragrance on its wings,
To mingle with the blisses of her dream;
This Summer wind, full of delicious sweets—
Bearing such perfume on its waving wings—
What was this Summer wind so full of sweets?

The maiden wandered in the Autumn wood,
The crisp red leaves rustled beneath her feet—
Those fairy, delicate, and wayward feet;
The frost had come, and with its chilly hand
Painted the forest in gay, gorgeous hues.
So had a frost fell on the lovely girl,
And made her radiance more splendid still—

Brighter and redder than the reddest leaf
Was the wild crimson of her burning cheek;
Her lip was restless as the quivering leaves,
And moaned and muttered as the forest did;
Her eyes were clearer than the azure sky,
And changing as the glitter of a star
In ocean depths, and brilliant as the sun.
As the green leaves were withered in a night,
So were her hopes changed to this gay despair;
At times she sang a low and pleasant song,
Then moaned and murmured as she hurried on
With quick, irregular steps and clasped hands;
And ever, as she walked, the Autumn wind
Swept past her with a mutter like her own—
And tore the bright leaves rustling from the bough—
And bore her golden hair upon its wings,
Far backward with its glittering length of beauty—
Or held her black dress with a trembling hand—
Or sighed in echo to her broken sigh—
Or sang and murmured, when her mood was soft—
Or moaned a wild reply unto her madness;
This mad and wayward maiden, and this wind,
As mad and wayward, hurried through the wood.
Oh, Autumn wind, as sweetly, sadly wild
As that fair creature wandering through the grove—
What was this Autumn wind so sadly wild?

The maiden stood alone in the cold night;
The sweetly pensive moon so shining fair,
Sent silvery messengers to learn her fate;
Her face was white like marble, and as still—
Her lip was motionless, and fixed, and pale—
And only those large, gleaming, beautiful eyes
Told that the heart yet shuddered in her breast.
One small, thin hand held tightly in its grasp
The robe of black unto her freezing breast,
Cold! intense cold! and yet she shivered not,
But stood with those wild eyes upon the moon—

On that lone plain a living, dying thing—
So frozen, beautiful, and strangely wild!
What pitied her? not the fierce Winter wind,
That howled and shrieked into her heedless ear,
And tore her garments frail, and pierced her frame,
Her very heart, with its sharp arctic spears!
Cold! bitter cold!—and yet she shivered not—
But slowly, slowly sank upon the earth,
While slowly, slowly closed those wild bright eyes,
And that pale form was frozen into death.
What did the cruel wind? it fled away,
And in its dark remorse called up the clouds
To vail the placid face of the pure moon,
Looking so solemn and so angel-like,
Then bade them weave a shroud—and thick and fast
The snowy flakes hurried through the dim air,
And lay all softly in a mantle white
Above the beautiful, dead, frozen clay.
Oh, cruel Winter wind that shrieked and howled,
And chilled the heart of earth's most lovely one—
What was this Winter wind that shrieked and howled?

A ROMANCE.

A HAUGHTY son of chivalry,
Handsome and proud and bold was he,
        Guy Mathers, of a noble line;
Fond of the field, and fond of the flood,
Fond of the hunt in the dark greenwood,
        And fond of good old wine

Was he, I said; alas, no more
Gallops his steed the country o'er,

Or sounds his heart-felt merriment.
Fled his mirthful soul and gallant mien,
Dim his eagle eye and good sword keen,
His haughty spirit bent.

Now what to work this change befell
The noble knight my song would tell,
Though wild and sad the tale will be—
Wild and sad as the spirits that croon
Their dreary songs to the wintry moon,
From the frozen fallow lea.

Guy Mathers loved a gentle maid—
Morna McDunn her name was said;
She—fairer and purer than snow—
Tender as any sweet young flower—
Was spelled by the brave knight's words of power,
And his voice so soft and low.

She loved, as only maidens do
Whose souls are soft and hearts are true,
And whose suitors are brave and bold;
And she was loved with an old-time love,
That could neither falter, faint, nor rove,
Neither grow fickle or cold.

Many a long month came and went,
And now the day was almost spent,
The last to shine on them unwed,
When Guy o'er the lonely moorland rode,
Just when the deepening twilight showed
Faintly the way he led.

High beat his heart with happiness,
Thinking of Morna's sweet caress;
When suddenly, thrilling and high,
Piercing the silence through and through,
A cry of fear on the dark air flew—
A wild and agonized cry.

Guy Mather's heart was soft as brave,
Ready to soothe and quick to save;
A moment listened he,
Then turned he his noble courser's head,
And the way that his ears were pointed sped,
Spurring him gallantly.

On toward the forest rode the knight;
The moorland mist was rising white,
And the darkness gathering fast;
Yet those fearful cries kept on before,
Till the knight had galloped across the moor,
And the forest's edge was past.

Then paused he, for the sound was lost;
By fitful lights his path was crossed—
His sight was blinded with their glare;
His panting steed with shivering limbs,
And eyes ablaze with terrified gleams,
Was trembling like a hare.

Many a legend dark and wild,
The knight had heard of men beguiled
By syrens in deceitful guise;
But alway had he derided well
The power of fairy ban and spell,
And of priestly exorcise.

Yet now a something chilled his blood,
To see the lovely shape that stood
Beckoning him with jeweled hand—
A lady in robes of forest green,
Sparkling with every jewel's sheen,
And many a golden band.

Three times the lady becked and smiled;
Her burning eyes were strangely wild,

Yet sweet and gently gay her mien;
A white and varying radiance shone
From her brow and feet, and jeweled zone,
And her robe was bright between.

Guy Mathers gazed with eyes entranced,
Nor once from his her own she glanced,
But smiled, and gazed, and smiled again;
Then retreating slowly, backward fled,
And the knight against his will was led,
Striving to turn in vain.

Away through forests wild and drear,
The syren led the knight in fear,
Binding him fast with fairy spell—
But such strange scenes the knight beheld,
By the enchantress' magic spelled,
It behooves not me to tell.

Oh, sad to say, the bridal day
Hath dawned, and shone, and passed away
Without the bridal rite!
Young Morna pale and silent lies,
With clasped hands and closed eyes,
Covered from joy and light.

Ah, woe to all in that grand hall—
The bride is hid beneath the pall,
The laggard bridegroom fled;
Strange whispers pass from friend to friend,
And wrath and awe and sorrow blend
Above the sweet young dead.

Guy Mathers' name, a mark for shame,
Is cursed and blackened o'er with blame;

The kinsmen of the bride
Through all the land have couriers fleet,
Who, till the reprobate they meet,
For life and death must ride.

No mercy, none, shall there be shown—
Life only shall the sin atone—
The forfeit must be paid.
Their pride is bent, their hearts are broke,
Guy Mathers gave the fatal stroke—
Their stern decree is made!

Alas, their hate! who at their gate
Is standing in such high debate?
Guy Mathers—it is he;
So changed, the porter knew him not—
But cursed him in his anger hot
For knocking noisily.

God help poor Guy! he knows not why
The brothers rush with angry eye
To bare the shining blade.
How could he guess how Morna died—
His darling one, his promised bride—
How could he think her dead?

How could he guess the strange distress,
The deep, unstinted bitterness
And shame that he must meet?
But hastened he the tale to tell
Of what adventures strange befell
His charmed and spelled feet.

Each brother staid his lifted blade
And listened to the tale he said,
And how his wild despair
Maddened at times his burning brain—
And yet he strove and strove in vain
To free him from the snare.

Each face grew pale to hear the tale—
Each lip to make reply did fail,
When Guy to see his bride
Demanded, with impatient haste,
Though faint and ill from lengthened fast,
And long and toilsome ride.

None dared to say how prone she lay,
And cold and senseless was her clay;
But gazed in silent dread,
And answered not, to his surprise,
Save with their mute and straining eyes,
To tell him she was dead.

And yet too soon his woe was known—
Guy fell into a fearful swoon,
Then wildly woke to rave;
And thence when reason came again,
To crave one last, last look in vain—
His love was in her grave.

Now years have fled since she was dead,
But young Guy Mathers never wed—
His heart was broken then;
And never since that fatal day
Mixes he with the young and gay,
Or holds converse with men.

THE SETTING SUN.

THE sun sank down, a crimson ball,
  In the sad, waveless sea of night;
A sullen gloom was over all,
  Streaked with that strange and fiery light.

The tide of twilight slowly rose,
  Tinged with the same unhappy glare,
And all the stars' sweet silver glows
  Were lost in the thick, vaporous air.

A moment, ere in sadness down
  The sun sank red and silently,
His forehead with its fiery crown
  Shone wild and lurid o'er the sea.

So in the black sea of despair,
  Sullen and fiery sank my heart,
And hot and glowing from the air
  Of hope and beauty did depart.

Sullen and hot my heart sank low,
  And its red, wild, and sickly glare
Glowed as a maniac's eyes will glow
  From out black brows and hanging hair.

As one by one the sun's red gleams
  Died out upon the surging sea,
So passion's once delightful dreams
  Within my breast died sullenly.

I watched the long and hopeless night—
  The storm furled up its pinions black—
The sun rose sweet, and fresh, and bright—
  The tide of twilight murmured back!

But from its sea of endless night
  My mad heart never rose again;
Long looked I for one gleam of light,
  But kept a desolate watch in vain.

Cold, dark, and senseless, still it lies
  Within a black and waveless sea,
In splendor never more to rise,
  And shine in love and melody.

TO ———.

The whole of this June day replete with roses,
  Replete with perfume, loveliness, and bloom,
From dewy morn till sunset's portal closes,
  From twilight till the midnight's starry gloom,
I offer up to thee, my loved and only—
  I offer up to thee my thoughts and dreams,
And though alone, I can not then be lonely
  While thus thy memory, like thy presence, seems.

All this soft sunshine through the white clouds glowing—
  All this faint fragrance of the summer air—
All this sweet melody around me flowing
  Of birds and breezes—all these blossoms fair—
This nameless influence of June's witching beauty
  That thrills my pulses like old golden wine,
With a half wish that I could deem it duty,
  And a sad joy, I offer on thy shrine.

My heart is full of tears that well up slowly,
  And fall upon the breast from whence they stole;
A placid sorrow, made by patience holy,
  Sits with bowed forehead in my silent soul!

The sunshine through the snowy clouds is stealing
  Like a bride's glances through her bridal vail,
And so Hope glances through the shadowy feeling
  That wraps it in a mantle soft and pale!

Oh, something in my heart pines on forever—
  A wish, a want, a yearning still the same;
And when to question it I make endeavor,
  The voice within me answers back thy name;
Oh, something in my heart moans on forever—
  With a low sound that haunts me night and day!
And when to question it I make endeavor,
  Alone—alone—alone! it seems to say.

But now, to-day, I hardly feel the pining—
  The moaning of my heart is almost still—
For thy dear presence all around is shining,
  Thy spirit all this loneliness doth fill!
I see thee, and I hear thee, and I know thee—
  Though far away, I recognize thee near!
This bright June beauty, so like thine, doth show thee
  Seen, yet impalpable, still lingering here.

The locust blossoms whitely wave and sparkle,
  Tossing their chalices upon the breeze,
Filled with the dewy drops that burn and darkle
  As they wave in and out among the trees.
Oh, these sweet locust-blossoms, tuned to dances,
  In their white beauty yearning toward the sky,
Are only like thy many graceful fancies,
  Restlessly beautiful, and pure, and high!

This brightness in the air, subdued and tender,
  Is like the presence of thy radiant eyes;
And yon white cloud that glows with a soft splendor—
  Such a young glory on thy forehead lies,

The waving of the spray in its sweet motion
 Is like the flowing of thy graceful hair!
Therefore for these I cherish a devotion,
 That more than admiration of the fair.

But most, this lonely day, I'm thrilled and haunted
 By this strange murmuring music in the trees—
Of all earth's melody the most enchanted—
 This whispering of the leaflets and the breeze;
Oh! I am haunted—haunted by its sweetness;
 It is so like thine own low, loving tone—
It fills my ear with music to repleteness,
 And fills my soul with harmony alone!

Yes, it is like thy voice, and like it only—
 Thy whispering, soothing, and mysterious voice!
It charms me from my sorrow wild and lonely—
 My heart at its low murmur doth rejoice;
It seems to whisper my own name unto me,
 As thou didst whisper it days long flown—
It seems to call on me and bless and woo me
 With tender dream, and thought, and yearning tone.

Ah! softly move the trees! and toward me bending,
 They seem to woo me to their graceful arms;
The music and the motion sweetly blending,
 Bewilder and allure me with their charms!
They seem to promise me a true affection,
 A pity for my loneliness and grief—
A care, a love, a beautiful protection,
 A sleep where weariness may find relief.

The sky is beauty and the air is sweetness—
 The shining clouds like billows melt away;
The earth hath robed herself with love's completeness
 This rosy, musical, and fragrant day.

I'm borne away upon its pinions golden,
To other times and scenes than these around—
My soul is floating upon mem'ries olden,
To a past world of feeling more profound—

To a past world seen with a young girl's vision—
Rose-tinted and gold-lighted Paradise!
Full of soft music and of paths elysian,
Lit even by the most bewildering skies—
By day unclouded, and by evening glowing
With the wild flashes of the mystic stars,
While 'neath their glory rivers ever flowing,
Ring molten notes of gold through silver bars!

In this past world, where thou and I, as fated,
Met by the dim, deep fountain of first love—
Drank from one cup with thrilling nectar freighted—
Then, with the angels smiling from above,
And roses in our path, and bosoms thrilling,
Together wandered through this Eden-land,
Our souls with beauty and with passion filling,
Led by a chain of light, linked hand in hand!

In this past world, where the first storm burst o'er us,
And wrapped us up in terror and surprise—
And tore our clinging hands apart and bore us
Far from each other and our paradise—
And left us weak and wasted, sad and lonely,
Calling upon each other through the gloom—
Yet finding not and hearing echoes only,
Treading on thorns instead of velvet bloom!

Upon one errand since that fatal hour
Does my faint spirit through the wide earth roam;
Nerving its wing with hope's mysterious power,
To find thee, lost one, and to bring thee home.

O beautiful as light! and brave and tender!
  Come back—come back to me! my soul doth cry;
But no reply thy distant soul doth render,
  And time creeps onward slowly, wearily.

Now all the sky in radiant beauty blushes—
  The golden sun woos the soft-swelling sea—
The west grows crimson and the far east flushes—
  Oped are the portals of Eternity!
And this June day, her golden tresses streaming,
  Her fair face and bright glances backward cast,
Her garments floating and her forehead beaming,
  Steps through the gorgeous gate to wed the Past.

Twilight is here; and now begins the throbbing,
  Wild, and no more subdued, of my dark heart;
The shadowy stillness listens to my sobbing,
  Broken, and faint, and bitter; hot tears start
Large, slow, and fiery, from their founts unbidden,
  And anguish frets and fevers my bent brow;
The language of my grief, from daylight hidden,
  Finds its own utterance and expression now.

O there is something soothing in the splendor
  Of the calm, shining, and most holy stars!
To me they ever have been true and tender,
  Leaning from out their silver-sparkling cars,
To smile upon me in my moods of madness,
  To hush my troubled thoughts and trance my tears,
To turn my anguish into softer sadness,
  And fill me with sweet hopes in place of fears.

I sob no more, but sit and mark them stealing
  From their blue-draperied chambers in the sky—
The many and the many still revealing
  Their placid foreheads from their homes on high;

I see them with their still and reverent faces,
  Come out to watch the earth in its fair sleep—
And bless them, smiling in their shining places,
  For the calm guard that pleasantly they keep.

We used to sit and watch the shining heaven,
  While locust-blossoms tossed upon the breeze—
We used to muse upon the "Pleiad seven,"
  And whisper thrilling words on nights like these!
The stars are here; the sounds to which I listen
  Are those that used to be to us so dear—
The roses sigh—the wet leaves wave and glisten—
  All have come back!—but thou—*thou art not here!*

THE POET'S COMPLAINT.

Out upon these flowing lines,
  And these words of dainty fashion,
When my chained heart pants and pines,
  And my soul consumes with passion!
Shall I make a low complaint,
  In words soft as flowers shutting?
Sure my madness is not faint,
  And my thoughts like knives are cutting!
Oh! my grief is nothing kind—
  Nothing pitiful or tender,
To be moved from out my mind
  By the evening's solemn splendor!
In the restlessness of fear
  I can see but phantoms only,
And I cry out sharp and clear,
  "I am lonely—I am lonely!"

I cry out in my dread—
  "Love and Beauty, do not shun me!"
But they long ago have fled,
  And my fear grows wild upon me;
'Tis the greatest wrong the dead,
  Loving, dying, e'er have done me!
'Tis the greatest wrong the world
  In its selfishness hath wrought me—
A kind and caring world
  From this darkness would have brought me—
When they knew I had a soul
  Which was full of dreams of beauty,
And a heart that spurned control,
  Save of love and loving duty—
And a spirit warm and bright,
  And a fancy most ethereal—
And an eye that loves the light,
  Falling over forms aerial—
And an ear that loves sweet sound,
  Such as ringing human laughter,
Such as heart-strings, so profound,
  Listening for the echo after!
Was it not a mighty wrong
  That they closed their golden portals,
Shutting me out from the throng
  Of each-other-seeking mortals?
Golden portals? I said well!
  They are golden portals truly!
We all know their value well,
  And appreciate them duly;
And had I a golden key,
  I could swing the hinges golden,
And could glide beyond and see
  All that the joy within enfolden.
But the world owes me a debt
  Which, if rightly it would render,
Would my happy spirit let
  Into happiness and splendor;

For all day I've sat and sang
  Underneath the shining arches;
And my solemn numbers rang
  With death's grand and stately marches—
And with songs of youthful love,
  Of despair and passion pleading,
Of the angels up above—
  Of lone hearts bereft and bleeding—
Of the rivers—of the sea—
  Of the trees in beauty waving—
Of the cunning melody
  Brooklets make, the pebbles laving!—
Of the sunset crimson-bright—
  Of the fearful roll of thunder—
Of the torrents in their might,
  And the caverns wrapped in wonder!—
Of the children in their mirth,
  And the lovers in their gladness—
Of the beauty of the earth—
  Of my lone self in my sadness!—
Looking through the golden bars
  With a spirit wildly yearning—
Seeing eyes as bright as stars,
  Ever to the singer turning.
Many widows clothed in woe,
  As I sang beneath the arches,
Came and listened to the flow
  Of the solemn-rolling marches;
Many maidens lingered near,
  With their cheeks and bosoms glowing,
And their young eyes shining clear,
  And their glorious tresses flowing,
While I sang of young love blest
  With a passion and a power
Rent from out my darkened breast,
  Like the lightning from a shower;
Many murmured words of praise,
  Smiling softly on each other

As they listened to the lays
  Which my bosom could not smother!—
Smiling in each other's eyes,
  But upon the singer never!
Murmuring sweet words of surprise,
  Wishing *I* might sing forever!
Alas! no one took my hand,
  No one led me through the portals
In among the social band
  Of each-other-seeking mortals!
When I sang of soft attire,
  No one cared that mine was tattered—
When I praised the silver lyre,
  No one saw that mine was shattered—
When I told of youthful glee,
  And of graceful-moving dances,
Of the gushing melody,
  And the sweetly loving glances—
No one saw how *I* was barred
  From the gliding and the dancing;
And no deep eye, darkling, cared
  That I wept its careless glancing;
When I sang of love divine
  With a passionate voice-like weeping,
No heart answered back to mine—
  Mine—its lonely vigil keeping.
And the twilight now is here—
  I am lonely—I am lonely!
And I almost shrink with fear
  With the shadows round me only;
My spirit makes one cry—
  One great cry of fear and sorrow!
The cold stars up in the sky
  Promise nothing for the morrow.
My mind trembles on the verge
  Of the seething sea of madness—
I can hear its frantic surge—
  Farewell! love and hope and gladness!

Farewell! cold and cruel world!
I have lost myself in terror—
In the sweeping sea I'm hurled
For what, God, what fatal error?

FRAGMENT.

I'll tell you what I heard, one starry night,
That made me love the sea, if you will listen.
The inner glow of the warm stars was shut,
And a rare brilliancy, cold and intense,
Shone from their covered foreheads; and this light
Seemed splintered into slender spears of ice,
Piercing the atmosphere with sparkling points.
You shudder, dainty love, for you were made
To pillow your young, Oriental cheek
On the invisible down of roses' leaves;
But I wear Arctic armor, and ne'er woo
The perfumed breeze of your enchanted land,
To rock my stories into numbers sweet.
There was a restless yearning in my heart,
That night of bitter cold and beauty wild,
That made me dare the challenge of the frost;
And, binding my sure skates to my swift feet,
I fled from hearth and home, music and love,
And stood alone upon the frozen lake:
Nothing around me but the lifeless ice—
Nothing above me but the starry space—
Nothing below me but the prisoned deep;
With forehead cold as the eternal stars,
And folded arms upon a heaveless breast,
I stood alone, the queen of my own passions!
Yet did the iron scepter of my will
Scarcely control those wild and powerful slaves,
Nor the imperial crown of pride prevent

Their taunting, and their burning, and their scorn.
Like a volcano, wrapped in mantling snow,
I stood beneath the sapphire-sparkling sky,
And lifted up my brow in silent pride.
A loneliness, as piercing as the cold,
Came down from heaven, and circled me about,
And with a subtile power compressed the air,
'Till the strong ice seemed crackling 'neath its weight.
You never knew, dear, Oriental child,
With that red, tremulous lip and loving eye,
And those dark lashes, that warm, crimson cheek,
And soft, white, throbbing bosom and quick tears—
You never knew the pining and the want,
The one-absorbing wish for—sympathy!
For every thing doth sympathize with thee, sweet love—
These rosy-tinted lamps, this soft perfume,
These shining stars, these white and golden flowers,
And every eye that catches your dear glance,
And every ear that drinks your musical tone,
And every heart that melts beneath your smile,
Or saddens at your tears—all, *all* are yours,
A part of your existence and yourself!
The only air that you can breathe and live
Is full of this sweet essence of yourself—
This beautiful and subtile sympathy!
As dropping water takes a spheral form,
All things around thee shape themselves to thee;
But I was born beneath some comet-star,
Some wild, ungoverned world of God's great space,
Whose fatal influence forever draws
My wayward spirit from love's circling sphere
Into strange labyrinths of loneliness!
There is no magnet in my polar breast
To draw about me hearts in sweet communion;
But ever burns within me one desire
To throw aside the chains that bind me here,
And fling my spirit on the universe,
That it, perchance, within that mighty scope

May meet its mate. 'Twas this desire, longing,
Power, or fatality, that sent me forth
On my swift skates, to dare the bitter cold,
The pathless ice, and the night's solitude.
Alone! as ever and forever, yet alone!
The golden stars were bright, but loved me not!
There was not even a shadow at my feet,
To be a little like my lonely self,
And not a leaf to make a quivering sound
In answer to the moaning of my soul.
I said I was alone—ha! what was that
Made answer to the voice within my soul?
I threw myself upon the moveless ice—
I clasped it with my arms, and laid my ear
Close to its chilly bosom, and I heard
A sound that thrilled me with a blissful awe:
A sympathy! a spirit! a communion!
Within that prison of unfeeling ice,
Shut up in darkness, mad with agony,
The spirit of the sea was bound and held!
I heard it—O I heard it, and I wept,
And loved it with a strange and passionate love!
I heard its hollow cry, its mighty moan—
I heard it dash its forehead on the walls
Which kept it from the starlight and the air—
I felt it shudder, and I shuddered too!
It shrieked, and from my lips a fearful shriek
Rang on the darkness—I could not repress it!
It seemed to sob, and I sobbed like a child!
I whispered to it through the cruel ice!
I felt the bliss—the great and mighty joy—
The solemn rapture—the ineffable power—
The charm—the spell—the grandeur—the delight—
The fullness and the perfectness of love!
Dear, tender spirit, in your happy heart
Lives no conception of my wild emotion!
No drooping leaves upon a slender tree
Were ever so much swayed by the wind's touch

As was my soul by each wail of woe,
Bursting beneath me from a mighty breast!
It, too, was chained and restless—in its cry
The moaning of *my* spirit found a voice—
I was no more alone!—at last—*at last!*
There came an answer to my yearning soul!
When I rose up again from the cold ice,
And turned my tearful eyes to the great sky,
In every star there burned a mystic fire,
And a rich radiance melted through the blue,
As soft as thine own eyes, my dear gazelle.

THE FIELD OF LILIES.

A field of lilies white
Bent down and crimsoned faintly in the light,
That golden, warm, and bright
From the sweet sunset came,
And touched them with a quivering lip of flame.

The angel of white hands,
Who kept the gates of heaven with his commands,
Led forth the radiant bands,
Who still, and bright, and fair,
Kept earth each night in safety by their prayer.

With soft and silent face—
Each wearing still their paradisal grace—
They stept out to their place!
Forth came the angel stars.
Through heaven's shining and soft sapphire bars.

They stood in the great skies,
And turned upon the earth their sparkling eyes;
Then something of surprise
Over one angel came—
He looked upon a lily touched with flame!

A last faint crimson dart,
With a soft thrill pierced the dear lily's heart,
As lingeringly apart,
A beam did trembling wait
Till the *white-handed* closed the western gate.

The lily bent to rest
And shutting the soft glory in her breast,
Dreamed of the radiant west—
The bright star knew her dreams
And blessed her with his sweetest shining beams.

The angel restless grew!
The lily soul had won that passionate hue,
So beautiful and true;
He said, "She needs my care—
In heaven there comes no woe—who needs me there?"

With a swift shining sweep,
His golden wings flashed through the azure deep
Of air, in night asleep;
Down to the earth he passed,
Hovering till his dear lily slumbered fast.

He saw her sweetly rest—
And closer, closer to his angel breast
His radiant wings he pressed—
And nearer, nearer crept—
And stole into her bosom while she slept!

Thus while he sparkling lies,
Smiles broke out 'neath the flower's folded eyes—
She dreamed of paradise!
She saw its golden streams,
And music melted through her blissful dreams.

At morn, awake she sprang,
While through her soul delicious chimings rang—
As though its visions sang!
What meant those quiverings?
Within her bosom *felt* she angel wings.

She sang—sweet words—untaught!
Deep revelations to her heart were brought,
With pain and pleasure fraught—
Tears with her singing blent!
Ah! tears with stars on earth are ever sent!

Men wandered with delight,
Amid this field of lilies pure and white;
A dew-drop, soft and bright,
Lay in each snowy breast,
As the bright beauty sparkles in the west.

This lily bent so low,
She nearly hid the angel-star's rich glow—
Men's gazes shamed her so;
They would not, could not hear
That rapt, wild music, passionate and clear.

They had no prophet-gaze—
They did not gather 'round in glad amaze,
To wonder and to praise;
They wore the dimming vail—
To *them* the angel was a dew-drop pale.

Through all that wondrous day
She thrilled and wept, and sang and pined away—
Yet—"wherefore?"—none would say.
Her longings were repressed—
Men could not see the angel in her breast!

She would not give again,
For all the dew-drops on that lovely plain,
Her wonder, bliss, and pain—
Yet, O mistaken star!
Thy lily when alone was happier far!

The angel saw the worth
(Sighing that *she* was not of heavenly birth)
Of genius upon earth—
Had he no power to save
The lily from an earthly, pitiless grave?

He waited till the night,
And when she dreamed, he spread his wings of light,
And from its robe of white
He bore her soul along,
And placed it in the outer Band of Song.

THE END.

Extracts from Reviews.

THESE graceful, spirited, and brilliant poetesses.—*New York Tribune.*

TWIN-GEMS fit to sparkle in the most regal tiara that Literature has yet worn in any part of the American continent.—*Cincinnati Columbian.*

THEY evidently write with great facility, with a fine command of poetical language, and a fancy singularly rich in apt and various illustration.—*Rufus W. Griswold.*

THESE unusually gifted ladies have given the highest evidences of superiority as poets. Their articles have appeared in various journals, but mainly in the Message Bird and Home Journal of New York.—*Racine Whig.*

THEIR contributions to Willis's "Home Journal" prove them to be real poets—*born poets*—of the unmistakable stamp. The "Post-Boy's Song" is worthy of Mrs. Norton or L. E. L. Others are full of the divinest fire of the muse.—*New Orleans Delta.*

THE Misses Fuller—particularly the younger of the sisters, who has written much for the "Home Journal," edited by Gen. Morris and N. P. Willis, under the signature of "Singing Sybil"—have an unusual degree of grace and imagination.—*Washington Union.*

OHIO is furnishing the Union with its best poetry. The Misses Fuller, when the capital is located at Cincinnati, will be knocking at its doors, to be crowned, as Petrarch was in Rome. We are proud of their genius, and confident of their triumphs.—*Ohio State Journal.*

THE qualities of their personal and social character are as attractive as their mental gifts are extraordinary. Good and kindly and pure as they are intellectual and accomplished, their writings will be found to deserve as warm a sympathy from the hearts of the virtuous as the admiration which they will receive from the judgments of the discerning.—*Detroit Tribune.*

THESE sister-poets are "stars of the West," as many of our journals call them, and are already enviably known to the great literary world, although young and just balancing upon the threshold of womanhood. Some of their productions have been widely republished, and have found a place in the English press. These sisters are undoubtedly destined to stand in the front rank with our American authors.—*Southern Christian Advocate.*

FRANCIS and METTA, the young poet-sisters, are notable instances of what gifted mind can accomplish in winning distinction. Without the advantages of wealth, literary friends, or patrons, to give them a favorable introduction to the reading world—"cumbered with much serving" in lightening the domestic duties of an invalid mother, their girlhood has been as

> "Rippling run two limpid streams,
> Singing now through twilight shadows,
> Sparkling now in noonday beams."

Cleveland Herald.

WE suppose ourselves to be throwing no shade of disparagement upon any one in declaring that in "Singing Sybil," and her not less gifted sister, we discern more unquestionable marks of true genius, and a greater portion of the unmistakable inspiration of true poetic art than in any of the lady minstrels—delightful and splendid as some of them have been—that we have heretofore ushered to the applause of the public. One in spirit and equal in genius, these most interesting and brilliant ladies—both still in the earliest youth—are undoubtedly destined to occupy a very distinguished and permanent place among the native authors of this land.—*Home Journal.*

WE had formed a high opinion of the ability of both writers; but we own that this opinion had not prepared us for the development of so much genius as is recognizable in the work before us. In the poems of Frances Fuller we discover much of that self-relying executive energy which gives its character to the genius of Elizabeth Barrett, while, in fancy and pathos, Metta, the younger of the sisters, reminds us vividly of "L. E. L." Faults they both have, undoubtedly, which are the result of seclusion and individualism —the necessary growth of unfostered genius—but their originality sometimes reduces these to positive beauties. The worst of them are far preferable to the labored and sinless elegance of our literary *dilletanti.* It is not our intention here, nor is this the time, to discuss the merits of these young poetesses; but it is our place to assert to the American public the claims of their genius, as native-born, freshly-developed, and worthy of that nurture which should warm it into the luxuriant beauty that it is capable of attaining.—*Message Bird, New York.*

Colton's Three Years in California.

THREE YEARS IN CALIFORNIA.

BY REV. WALTER COLTON, U. S. N.,

LATE ALCALDE OF MONTEREY.

WITH NUMEROUS ILLUSTRATIONS.

"A rare work this for ability, interest, information, mirth, and as the most recent and most authentic history of California, since it came under the American flag. It contains excellent portraits of Messrs. Sutter, Larkin, Fremont, Gwinn, Wright, and Snyder, with numerous and humorous illustrations; a list of the members of the Convention which organized the State of California; a chart of the '*Declaration of Rights*,' with *fac-similes* of the signatures, &c. Nothing of interest to the public in the rapid growth of this new world, its towns, villages, and settlements, its gold digging, gold explorations, &c., escapes the notice of the author; and the pictures he has given of California life and manners are at the same time graphic, instructive, and often in the most provoking degree mirthful."—*National Intelligencer.*

"It is the best history of California that has appeared, and will prove as instructive as it is interesting and provocative of mirth."—*Rochester Democrat.*

"This work is an authentic history of California, from the time it came under the flag of the United States down to this present, explorations, new settlements, and gold diggings. While the reader is instructed on every page, he will laugh about a hundred if not a thousand times before he gets through this captivating volume, and though he sits alone in his chair. It is, in the first place, a book of fact; next to the remarkable and ludicrous peculiarities of California life and manners, are an incessant provocation to make one laugh; and the author being a poet, gives us a fine relish of that every now and then."—*Washington Republic.*

"The anticipations of those who expected from Mr. Colton a book about California at once reliable and entertaining, comprehensive and concise, instructive and lively—in fact, just what a work of the kind ought to be, but what a majority of the numerous accounts heretofore published are not—will be abundantly realized on perusal of this volume. Mr. Colton, besides possessing the various qualifications of an intelligent observer—a highly-cultivated mind, stored with ample material for comparison, in the fruits of years spent in travel in every part of the world, and intercourse with numerous peoples—enjoyed peculiar advantages for becoming acquainted with California, in his long residence there; in his exalted official position, which made him the associate and counsellor of the highest functionaries in the province; in a philosophical disinterestedness, which, while it raised him above the scramble for treasure, enabled him calmly to survey the field of action, and describe the operations of the scramblers; and, finally, in an elevated personal character, which commanded the respect and won the confidence and regard of all classes of the people."—*Journal of Commerce.*

"It is the most instructive work on California we have seen."—*Commercial Advertiser.*

Colton's Three Years in California.

"It is certainly refreshing to find such a book as this one, after having vainly searched for something authentic, 'true to nature,' and at the same time *readable*, among the thousands which have been issued from the prolific press since the discovery of 'El Dorado.' We hail it as almost as dear a treasure as would be the discovery of a rich 'placer,' were we upon the veritable soil of California. We have stolen time during the past week to hastily glance over the pages of Mr. Colton's book, and our opinion, before very high, because of the encomiums universally bestowed upon it by our contemporaries, has rather been increased, certainly not diminished, and we think a more careful perusal will well repay. Our longing upon this point has been satiated, and we can safely say that we have gained more of a knowledge of California, as it was before, and as it has been since the discovery of gold in its soil." —*Syracuse Journal.*

"Mr. Colton is one of the most agreeable of American writers. His ideas flow as it were *spontaneously*—one moment grave, then gay. One moment we feel, while reading his books, like weeping at some well-drawn picture, and the next, we can hardly keep from splitting our sides with laughter, at some brilliant, mirth-provoking expression."—*Republican Advocate.*

"There never was a better illustration of the saying, that 'Truth is stranger than fiction,' than is found in this narrative. Truly, the *real* is a more wonderful world than the *ideal*. When the writer of this interesting and delightful book landed at San Francisco, California was a dependency of the Republic of Mexico; but when he left it, in all but in name, it was a State of the American Union: now it is one. Its newly risen, but glorious star is shining in the bright constellation where clusters the stars of its sister States; its senators and representatives are sitting with those of the other members of the Confederacy in the halls of the national legislature, at Washington. The causes that have been so busily at work in producing this series of astonishing changes, are all truthfully detailed in this narrative, as they occurred from day to day, and as they came under the keen but discriminating observation of one who had the best opportunity of knowing, as well as the happiest manner of relating them. Any thing like an analysis of a volume so filled as this is with striking incidents, crowding one after another in such rapid succession, is impossible. As we read on from page to page, we become more and more interested, as the things which it records become more and more important, until we seem to partake of the wild enthusiasm that must have been felt by the immediate actors in these imposing but exciting scenes of a most eventful drama. For once the sober dignity of history is compelled to put on the airs and charms of romance. This beautiful volume can be read with mingled pleasure and profit by all who wish to get correct ideas of the golden land, towards which all eyes are now turned."—*Niagara Democrat.*

"A full account of the appearance of that curious disease, 'the gold fever,' from the first scattering cases up to the time when the whole population was infected, is admirably given, with strange and amusing illustrations of individual attacks. For the purpose of fully studying the disease, the worthy alcalde himself repaired to the mines, and observed it in all its glory. His descriptions, therefore, must be perfect, from having been made upon the spot. The well-known ability and position of the author, fitted him admirably to observe and note passing events in a territory of such vast importance; and the reader may turn to the journal of Mr. Colton for an accurate chronicle of events.

"From humor, statistics, description, historical narrative, mining, agricultural and political information, this book is calculated to attract every class of readers."—*Washington Union.*

Colton's Deck and Port.

DECK AND PORT;

OR,

INCIDENTS OF A CRUISE IN THE UNITED STATES FRIGATE CONGRESS TO CALIFORNIA:

With Sketches of RIO JANEIRO, VALPARAISO, LIMA, HONOLULU, and SAN FRANCISCO. By Rev. WALTER COLTON, U. S. N., late Alcalde of Monterey. Illustrated with Engravings. 1 vol. 12mo.

"We are indebted to the publishers for one of the most delightful books we have received in an age. Though professedly commenced 'more as the whim of the hour, than any purpose connected with the public press,' the polished and gifted author has infused so much of spirit and sentiment into the various daily 'jottings,' as to render the volume one series of delightful conversations. The sketches of the different cities visited are beautifully executed, and printed in tints."—*Phila. Saturday Courier.*

"There are elements of popularity and interest enough in this handsome volume to make a market for a dozen. California is a magic word in these days; and those upon whom it does not operate with sufficient power to tear them away from home, friends, and health at home, feel its influence quite enough to devour every thing that relates to it. This work is by far the most methodical, satisfactory, and graphic description of El Dorado, and the way thither, that has yet appeared. Mr. Colton will be remembered by those who read his admirable 'Ship and Shore' as a most lively, humorous, and sketchy writer; and his best qualities are brought into play in this work. The amount of valuable information on which his pleasant sketches are based, is very great. The value of the book is also greatly increased by the illustrations it contains. There are a large number of sketches of scenes and places, drawn by Mr. Colton, beautifully engraved, and printed in colors, which are fine works of art, and give a vivid idea of the places visited. It is a work whose literary merit, attractive form, and most interesting matter, will make it highly popular."—*N. Y. Evangelist.*

"This is unquestionably one of the most interesting books that has been issued from the American press the present year. We have never read a book that pleased us more. Possessing a brilliant imagination, the author has painted, in glowing colors, a thousand pictures of the sea, night and storm, sunshine and calm. Every page is full of glowing thoughts, sublime truths, pure morals, and beautiful aphorisms. It is a book that will never be out of date—it is a gem that will become brighter every day. We predict that this volume will run through several editions."—*Pittsburg Morning Post.*

"This work is published in a beautiful style, and is full of highly interesting scenes and incidents, detailed by a master hand. It has been seldom that we have found a work more instructive, and at the same time so interesting as the one before us. To say any thing in praise of the author, would be useless. His fame is so well settled, that our opinion could neither raise it higher nor detract from its merits.

"Every thing related, is clothed in the rich garniture which is afforded by a well stored and well cultivated mind, governed by high moral principle. The whole tenor of the work, while it aims at instructive narration, is also calculated to impress upon the mind pure and elevated ideas, both of men and things.

"We have no hesitation in saying to all who want a *good*, *useful*, and interesting book, that they cannot do better than to secure a copy of this. It will richly repay a perusal."—*Massillon News.*

"His pen has the wand-like power of making the scenes which it describes live and move before the mind of the reader. We can cheerfully recommend this as a charming book, full of information and entertainment."—*Hartford Christian Secretary.*

Colton's Deck and Port.

"This volume, by the author of 'Ship and Shore,' is full of racy and original thoughts, clothed in language remarkable for its elegance and strength. The author has long been a wanderer over sea and land, and has noted, with a searching eye. the striking traits and usages of different nations. These he throws into a sketch, with that vivid light and shade which transport the scene almost palpably before your eyes. He knows the sailor thoroughly, and lets you into all the subtle springs of action which sway that generous and reckless being.—Skilled in prose, the author is yet in heart and soul a poet, and looks on nature with a poet's eye. The snatches of faultless verse which he has occasionally introduced into his pages, will arrest the attention of the reader. His wit, which sparkles out here and there, is free of all bitterness. His sentiments are expressed with frankness, firmness, and a self-relying spirit. The volume, graceful in itself, is ornamented with a striking portrait of Commodore Stockton, and with spirited prints of places and costumes described in its pages."—*National Intelligencer.*

"Those who want something fresh and interesting; something that will amuse and instruct at the same time, without being dull or wearisome—will find what they seek in this elegantly written and equally elegantly printed volume. The author possesses in an eminent degree the happy faculty of seizing on the most interesting occurrences, and drawing from them appropriate reflections on the general duties of life. He never misses an opportunity to teach a lesson, yet he never seems to seek for one."—*Niagara Democrat.*

"The contents, in a journal form, are full of lively incidents, written in a very pleasing style, and on the whole are so interesting, that one is very reluctant to lay the volume down. Few works of fiction could be more attractive in any respect. We doubt not that 'Deck and Port' will have a wide circulation."—*New Haven Palladium.*

"An agreeable diary of a voyage round 'the Horn,' in a man-of-war, by a Christian scholar and gentleman. We have seldom met with a book of travel so free from fuss and pretence. The note-worthy incidents of life at sea are jotted down, apparently as they rise, from day to day, in easy, natural prose, so that the reader soon feels himself quite at home on board a man-of-war, enjoying its society and scenes, and participating in the humor and sentiments of its 'floating population.' Sketches are given also of the various ports visited—Rio, Valparaiso, Lima, Honolulu, Monterey, San Francisco, &c.; and graphic illustrations are furnished by the engraver."—*Newark Daily Advertiser.*

"We have read a large portion of this work with great interest. It is written in a lively, graphic style; and recounts, in a very pleasing narrative, the incidents of a long and perilous voyage round Cape Horn, with descriptions of Valparaiso, Lima, Callao, San Francisco, &c.; their religion, manners, and customs. This book is one of the most readable of the season, the writer having attained the art of making the reader feel as though he were one of the party, and thus interested in all their toils, trials, perils, adventures, amusements, &c."—*Pres. Advocate.*

"Mr. Colton is an observing and ready writer; and his office on board of the ship afforded him every needed facility for obtaining a knowledge of the character of the men on board, and of the multitude of incidents of every hue that make up life in a ship. His is a free pen, and he writes with much facility of expression and elegance of taste; making one of the most agreeable volumes that has ever been written with reference to that interesting portion of the world."—*Worcester Palladium.*

"The author's situation as chaplain, together with his long connection with the navy, rendered him fully competent to give correct pictures of all we landsmen wish to know, while he excels in a graphic power particularly adapted to this kind of writing. His style is light and sketchy, having the freshness of a journal where the author had evidently each day dotted down what most arrested his own attention. Altogether, it is a capital view of sea life, and the liveliness of the style keeps the interest from flagging to the end. We predict for it an extensive circulation."—*Albany State Register.*

"The author's opportunities have been most ample for furnishing correct information in regard to the many interesting and ever-changing scenes that a person in the naval service is continually experiencing. His style is so pointed and free from that monotony which is too apt to find its way into such narratives, that we do not hesitate to predict for the book an extensive sale."—*Albany Daily Advertiser*

History of the Mexican War.

THE MEXICAN WAR:

A History of its Origin, with a detailed Account of the Victories which terminated in the surrender of the Capital, with the Official Despatches of the Generals. By EDWARD D. MANSFIELD, Esq Illustrated with numerous Engravings.

From the Philadelphia North American.

Mr. Mansfield is a writer of superior merit. His style is clear, nervous, and impressive, and, while he does not encumber his narrative with useless ornament, his illustrations are singularly apt and striking. A graduate of West Point, he is of course familiar with military operations; a close and well-read student, he has omitted no sources of information necessary to the purposes of his work; and a shrewd and investigating observer, he sees in events not alone their outward aspects, but the germs which they contain of future development. Thus qualified, it need hardly be said that his history of the war with Mexico deserves the amplest commendation.

From the New York Tribune.

A clear, comprehensive, and manly history of the war, is needed; and we are glad to find this desideratum supplied by Mr. Mansfield's work.

From the New York Courier and Enquirer.

This is really a history, and not an adventurer's pamphlet destined to live for the hour and then be forgotten. It is a volume of some 360 pages, carefully written, from authorities weighed and collated by an experienced writer, educated at West Point, and therefore imbued with a just spirit and sound views, illustrated by plans of the battles, and authenticated by the chief official despatches.

The whole campaign on the Rio Grande, and that, unequalled in brilliancy in any annals, from Vera Cruz to the city of Mexico, are unrolled before the eyes of the reader, and he follows through the spirited pages of the narrative, the daring bands so inferior—in every thing but indomitable will and unwavering self-reliance, and military skill and arms—to the hosts that opposed them, but opposed in vain.

We commend this book cordially to our readers.

From the Baptist Register, Utica.

The military studies of the talented editor of the Cincinnati Chronicle, admirably qualified him to give a truthful history of the stirring events connected with the unhappy war now raging with a sister republic; and though he declares in his preface that he felt no pleasure in tracing the causes, or in contemplating the progress and final consequences of the conflict, yet his graphic pages give proof of his ability and disposition to do justice to the important portion of our nation's history he has recorded. The very respectable house publishing the book, have done great credit to the author and his work, as well as to themselves, in the handsome style in which they have sent it forth.

VALUABLE MUSIC BOOKS.

Edited by Geo. Kingsley, Professor of Music—author of "Social Choir," "Sacred Choir," &c.

KINGSLEY'S JUVENILE CHOIR

A selection of the choicest melodies from the German, Italian, French, English, and American composers. Designed for public and private schools, and for young classes in academies and seminaries. Price 40 cts.

KINGSLEY'S YOUNG LADIES' HARP.

A selection of secular and sacred music, arranged in two and three parts, with a Piano Accompaniment. Designed for female seminaries, and the social circle. Price 75 cts.

KINGSLEY'S HARP OF DAVID.

A collection of Church Music, consisting of selections from the most distinguished composers, together with original pieces by the editor—also a progressive system of Elementary instruction for pupils. Price $1.00.

Extract of a Letter from Mr. Gilbert Combs, Principal of the Female Seminary, Philadelphia.

Among the numerous works now prepared for youth, few are worthy of taking a higher rank than Kingsley's Juvenile Choir. Arranged in a style calculated to enlist the youthful feelings, it is still free from common-place or imperfect harmonies It is chaste in style, simple and pure in sentiment, and vigorous in tone. Much of the music is original, and the favorite airs that are copied, are much improved in harmony and adaptation. * * * * * * A judicious teacher, with the aid of such a manual, can hardly fail to produce good scholars. * * *

From the Louisville Journal.

KINGSLEY'S JUVENILE CHOIR.—This is the title of a delightful little collection of vocal music for the use of children. The tunes are well selected, and there is a great deal of beautiful poetry which children will *feel*. It would be a treat to hear some of these songs sung by a school of sweet young voices. Music should be taught in every primary school. Nothing can be better for cultivating the taste and sweetening the affections. Men are too much inclined to believe that the only object in education is to enable the pupil to count up dollars and cents. They forget that there are other objects much more important than to make of man a good calculating machine.

From the Milwaukie Sentinel.

KINGSLEY'S HARP OF DAVID.—This is an excellent collection of Church Music, consisting of the best selections from distinguished composers, and a number of original pieces. It is compiled by George Kingsley, professor of music and author of "The Sacred Choir," &c. By way of preface, there is a very complete and intelligible elementary course of instruction in vocal music. The work is very neatly printed and got up, throughout, in excellent taste. It is not only a useful assistant for the choirs of churches, but may be introduced with advantage into the school-room and the family circle. It embraces 360 pages, and contains no less than 317 different tunes. We believe, indeed, that it is the most complete collection of Church Music now in print.

Miscellaneous Books.

POPE'S HOMER'S ILIAD. 32mo. sheep.

This edition of the translation of Homer is used not only as a volume for the Library, but as a text-book in grammar classes in Schools and Academies.

POLYMICRIAN NEW TESTAMENT. (Illustrated with Maps.)

This is the only edition of Polymicrian New Testament published in this country. It contains short explanatory Notes, and numerous references to illustrative and parallel passages, printed in a centre column.

WATTS ON THE IMPROVEMENT OF THE MIND. With Questions.

There is no book better adapted for the School Room, or more calculated to be useful to the youth of our country, than a familiar acquaintance with the sound instruction of this learned divine, given in this manual.

"An old substantial author in a new dress,—a little volume of 281 pages, in a neat but cheap form, worth its weight in gold; no sensible discriminating man would ever think of collecting a library without including this work. For a professing Christian to say that he has never read it, would argue that his reading had been superficial indeed. It is neither dry nor uninteresting, but it is filled with solid and useful truths." —*Western Paper.*

COLTON'S PUBLIC ECONOMY FOR THE UNITED STATES.

One Vol. 8vo.

"In this volume of 536 pages octavo, Mr. Colton, who is favorably known to the American public as the author of the 'Life of Clay,' the 'Junius Tracts,' and other popular works, has supplied the desideratum of a complete defence of the protective system, and an answer to the numerous works on the Free Trade side of the question. As far as we are able to judge from the opportunity we have had to examine the elaborate arguments of the author in the work before us, it appears to us that he has produced a work not only calculated to refute the points made by writers in favor of free trade, but sufficient to puzzle them to find ready answers to many of the positions he has taken. We rather think they will be disposed either to misrepresent him, or to pass over in silence some of his most potent arguments."—*New York Tribune.*

GOULD'S ABRIDGMENT OF ALISON'S EUROPE. One Vol. 8vo.

This work presents a comprehensive and perfect view of Europe during the stormy period from 1789 to 1815, in clear and perspicuous language, and in a beautiful style. Its publication supplies a desideratum in History, there being no work of a similar character attainable by the public, except at four times the expense. It is well adapted as a class-book in History for Colleges, Academies, and Schools, as well as for the general reader.

COLTON'S LIFE AND TIMES OF HENRY CLAY. In Two Vols. 8vo.

"Mr. Colton has done his work—a great work—bravely and well. This is the first successful life of Henry Clay yet written. This describes the man, not as a politician, orator, statesman, alone, but as all—and that honestly, candidly, thoughtfully, and the darkest and deepest passages intelligibly and philosophically. The chapters of his early life and personal character are beautiful, and the account of his political rise intensely interesting."—*Hunt's Merchant's Magazine.*

www.ingramcontent.com/pod-product-compliance
Lightning Source LLC
LaVergne TN
LVHW010235110826
845151LV00004B/1300

9781425525439